D0812579

THE DINOSAUR LIBRARY

Meat-Eating Dinosaurs
The Theropods

Thom Holmes and Laurie Holmes

Illustrated by Michael William Skrepnick

Series Advisor:
Dr. Peter Dodson
Professor of Veterinary Anatomy and Paleontology,
University of Pennsylvania
and
co-editor of *The Dinosauria*,
the leading reference used by dinosaur scientists

Enslow Publishers, Inc.

40 Industrial Road	PO Box 38
Box 398	Aldershot
Berkeley Heights, NJ 07922	Hants GU12 6BP
USA	UK

http://www.enslow.com

Library of Congress Cataloging-in-Publication Data

Holmes, Thom
    Meat-eating dinosaurs : the theropods / Thom Holmes and Laurie Holmes;
illustrated by Michael William Skrepnick.
      p. cm. — (The dinosaur library)
    Includes bibliographical references (p.) and index.
    ISBN 0-7660-1452-5
      1. Saurischia—Juvenile literature. [1. Dinosaurs. 2. Carnivores.] I. Holmes,
Laurie. II. Skrepnick, Michael William, ill. III. Title. IV. Title: Theropods. V. Series:
Holmes, Thom. Dinosaur Library
QE862.S3 H65   2001
567.912—dc21
                                    00-009329

Printed in the United States of America

10 9 8 7 6 5 4 3

To Our Readers: We have done our best to make sure all Internet addresses in this book were
active and appropriate when we went to press. However, the author and the publisher have
no control over and assume no liability for the material available on those Internet sites or on
other Web sites they may link to. Any comments or suggestions can be sent by e-mail to
comments@enslow.com or to the address on the back cover.

Illustration Credits: Michael William Skrepnick. Illustrations on p. 50 after Welles
1984a, Gilmore 1920, Paul 1988, Zhao and Currie 1993, and Bonaparte 1990;
p. 53 after Osborn 1912, Brochu 2000; p. 81 after Larson/Currie.

Photo Credits: © Corel Corporation, p. 14; © Digital Vision, Ltd., p. 30; Wayne
Grady, p. 4 (Thom Holmes); Thom Holmes, pp. 21, 22, 34, 64, 75, 83, 85, 89;
Shaina Holmes, p. 4 (Laurie Holmes); Michael Tropea, p. 5.

Cover Illustration: Michael William Skrepnick, originally published on *Dinosaur
Imagery, The Science of Lost Worlds and Jurassic Art—The Lazendorf Collection,*
Academic Press, 2000, ISBN 0-12-436590-6.

CONTENTS

ABOUT THE AUTHORS

Thom Holmes is a natural history writer specializing in dinosaur science. He has dug for dinosaurs with leading paleontologists in the United States, South America, and Egypt. He has collaborated with Dr. Peter Dodson on several dinosaur-related projects during the past fifteen years.

Laurie Holmes is a science writer and editor, as well as a reading specialist. It has been her privilege to associate with many of the world's leading dinosaur scientists and artists through her work with her husband, Thom. Originally a teacher, she maintains that she is still teaching by writing and editing books for young adults.

On a dig in Patagonia, Thom Holmes holds part of the skull bone of what is currently known as the largest theropod ever.

Thom Holmes

Laurie Holmes

AUTHORS' NOTE

Dinosaurs hold a special fascination for people all over the world. In writing *The Dinosaur Library*, we enjoyed sharing the knowledge that allows scientists to understand what dinosaurs were really like. You will learn about the differences that make groups of dinosaurs unique, as well as the many similarities that dinosaurs shared.

The Dinosaur Library series covers all the suborders of dinosaurs, from the meat-eating theropods, such as *Tyrannosaurus rex*, to the gigantic plant eaters. We hope you enjoy learning about these fascinating creatures that ruled the earth for 160 million years.

ABOUT THE ILLUSTRATOR

Michael William Skrepnick is an established paleo artist with a lifelong interest in dinosaurs. He has worked on newly described dinosaurs with a number of the world's leading paleontologists. His original artworks are found in a number of art collections and reproduced as museum murals, and in popular books, magazines, scientific journals, and television documentaries.  Michael lives and works in Alberta, Canada, close to some of the richest Upper Cretaceous dinosaur fossil localities in the world.

Paleo art is a field devoted to the reconstruction and life restoration of long extinct animals and their environments. Since we cannot observe dinosaurs (other than living birds) in nature, we may never truly know their habits, lifestyles, or the color of their skin. In addition, the fossil record provides only a fraction of the remains of a wide diversity of life on earth.

Many fairly complete skeletons of dinosaurs have been unearthed in recent history. Others are represented by as little as a fragment of a single fractured bone, an isolated tooth, or a footprint impressed in once-wet mud. It is still possible to create a reliable portrait of unique, previously unknown creatures, but the accuracy of the art depends on the following:

- The quality and amount of actual skeletal material of the specimen preserved
- Discussion and collaboration with a paleontologist familiar with the fossil material and locality from which it was excavated
- Observation and comparisons to the closest related living forms
- The technical abilities, skill, and disciplined vision of the artist

The resulting artwork can draw the viewer back in time into exotic worlds of the ancient.

TYRANNOSAURUS ATTACK

The old bull Tyrannosaurus *was huge and slow. The legs that had once propelled him to the quick attack now ached and creaked with age. His tail, still supported with powerful muscles to keep it straight, now seemed heavy as he stood peering out through an opening in the trees. He heaved a sour breath and sucked in another, holding it momentarily to keep himself still. At his advancing age, surprise was as important as the overpowering strength that he still had in his jaws.*

A small herd of edmontosaurs—duck-billed dinosaurs—was entering the clearing on the edge of the evergreen forest. In years past, this Tyrannosaurus *would have boldly pursued his next meal in the open. He would have strode defiantly into view and chased down his prey with the snapping reach of his deadly jaws. But now, unable to run as he once did, he hid in the thick of the forest, behind the low-hanging branch of a sprawling cypress tree. Had he sauntered into the clearing as in the old days, the duck-bills would surely have scattered immediately into the surrounding evergreens. And he would have gone hungry for another day.*

The fact that he hid downwind of his prey may not have been an accident. He had learned that he could smell his prey coming from a distance if the breeze was blowing from their direction. This allowed him to be aware of their presence even before seeing them. He poked his nose through the gnarled tree branches, making a little opening to watch the duckbills approaching. He pointed his nose in their direction, using the slightly overlapping vision of his eyes to pick them out. There were several in the group, some large, some small.

The duckbills were not yet aware of the Tyrannosaurus *spying on them. They moved cautiously, following a large female, who perked up and turned to study any sound that was out of the ordinary. The duckbills were nibbling on the small evergreens and fern trees at the edge of the forest. They came closer and closer to the hiding place of the* Tyrannosaurus.

There were eight edmontosaurs in the group. None had large head crests like those that honked so loudly when they were under attack. There were three adults and five juveniles. The first two adults walked with firm steps, waving their heavy tails from side to side with grace and power. They walked nearest the edge of the forest, using their large bodies to shield the young ones from danger that might possibly emerge from the woods. The young ones were half grown, about fifteen feet long.

Trailing somewhat behind the others was an old female. She walked slowly, gradually drifting farther and farther behind her companions. She appeared to be sick, walking with her head down, barely observing the world around her.

It was time for the Tyrannosaurus *to make his move. He was most interested in the young dinosaurs or one of the healthy adults. He inhaled again, holding his breath to remain still, pausing for the right moment. But before the duckbills had come close enough to ensure a kill, the old* Tyrannosaurus *wavered slightly and lost his balance, stepping out with his large foot. The twigs and dried cypress cones that blanketed the ground under the tree crinkled and snapped as he stepped on them. That was it, no time to wait. He lunged forward as quickly as he could, bursting through the low-hanging branches of the tree.*

At the sound of the snapping twigs, the first two adult duckbills quickly swung around to face the danger. The younger ones, having survived this kind of attack several times before, sped as fast as their legs could carry them away from the sound of the attacking tyrannosaur. The two adults swung their heavy tails around to ward off their foe.

The first tail missed the old Tyrannosaurus *entirely, but the second whipped him in the side, causing him to stagger sideways. His large foot claws quickly regained their grip and he lurched forward with his snapping jaws before the closest duckbill could whip its tail around again. His huge teeth caught the side of the duckbill and ripped several large gashes in its hide, but the duckbill leaped forward and out of danger, nearly causing the* Tyrannosaurus *to fall on his face.*

The two adults and young duckbills ran for safety, and the tyrannosaur, after rising up and steadying himself, felt the pain in

his aching legs and decided not to chase them. He had come close, tasted the blood of his prey, but could do no more.

Then the Tyrannosaurus remembered the old straggling duckbill. It was still in the clearing but stumbling weakly toward the trees. The tyrannosaur grunted in recognition and advanced as fast as he could toward his prey. He reached the old duckbill just as it was beginning to enter the woods. The tyrannosaur's arms were short—even too short to put food in his mouth—but they

were strong. He used the two claws on each hand to hook the duckbill in the side, holding it tight so that it could not get away. The duckbill tried to take steps, hoping to scramble away, but the strength of the tyrannosaur was too great. The duckbill let out a bellow of pain as the tyrannosaur closed its bone-crushing jaws on its neck. The tyrannosaur ate what it could, taking its time, then moved on and let the carrion eaters finish off the carcass.

Several days later, as the old Tyrannosaurus continued to

walk in the direction of the escaped duckbills, he detected the satisfying odor of a dead dinosaur. Just ahead, he came across the body of the adult duckbill he had bitten near the woods. It had died only hours before. The tyrannosaur often found its victims like this, days after having attacked them. The duckbill may have bled to death from its wounds. Or it may have died from an infection picked up from the bacteria in the tyrannosaur's bite. It made no difference now how the duckbill died. All the tyrannosaur knew was that his next meal would come from this carcass.

A group of small meat eaters called Troodon *("wounding tooth") had already begun pecking away at the five-ton body. The old* Tyrannosaurus *chased them away with a gesture of his head and a menacing grunt. He reached down with the four-foot expanse of his open mouth and bit into the fleshy leg of the dead duckbill, ripping the skin and meat away in huge chunks. He did not chew with his large, banana-shaped teeth. His teeth were sharp and did not have a grinding surface. Instead, he opened and closed his jaws repeatedly to shred the chunks of meat into smaller ones that he could swallow whole. He crushed bones in his mouth until they were small enough to swallow safely. With a full mouth, he raised his snout toward the sky and shook his head from side to side to shimmy the meal down his throat.*

As the Tyrannosaurus *got older and older, it would become unable to chase down its own prey. One day, he would rely on the kills of others for his meals. Then, when he died, it would be his turn to become a meal for others.*

Author's Note—The preceding dinosaur story is fiction but is based on scientific evidence and ideas suggested by paleontologists. You will find explanations to support these ideas in the chapters that follow. Use the following guide to find these references:

- Locomotion and speed: p. 59 (Theropod Speed)
- Scavenging versus hunting for prey: p. 71 (Hunters or Scavengers?)
- Methods of killing prey: pp. 72, 80 (Killing Tactics, Toxic Teeth)
- Chewing and eating: p. 39 (Theropod Skulls and Teeth)
- Diet: p. 80 (What Did They Eat?)
- Intelligence: p. 47 (Brains and Smarts)
- Senses of sight, smell, and hearing: p. 49 (Senses)

CHAPTER 1

DINOSAURS DEFINED

What are dinosaurs? Dinosaurs were reptiles, but they were a special kind that no longer exists. Many people assume that all dinosaurs were gigantic. Some confuse the dinosaurs with extinct reptiles that flew (the pterosaurs) and those that lived in the sea (e.g., plesiosaurs, ichthyosaurs, and mosasaurs). How does one know for sure whether a creature was a dinosaur or not?

Dinosaurs came in many shapes and sizes. Some were many times larger than the largest land animals alive today. Others were as small as chickens. Some were carnivores (they ate meat); others were herbivores (they ate mostly plants). Some walked on two legs, others on four legs. Yet, in spite of these vast differences, vertebrate paleontologists who study dinosaurs have identified many specific characteristics that allow them to classify dinosaurs as a group of related creatures, different from all others.

Dinosaurs lived only during the Mesozoic Era. The age of dinosaurs spanned from the Late Triassic Period, about 225 million years ago, to the Late Cretaceous Period, some 65 million years ago. Fossils dating from before or after that time were not dinosaurs. This rule also means that all dinosaurs are *extinct.* Today's birds, however, are believed to be modern relatives of the dinosaurs.

Dinosaurs were a special kind of reptile. Dinosaurs had basic characteristics common to all reptiles. They had a backbone and scaly skin, and they laid eggs. They were also the ancestors of birds, with some showing birdlike features such as clawed feet, hollow bones, and even feathers.

Dinosaurs were land animals. Reptiles adapted for flying or living in the water were present at the same time as the dinosaurs, but they were *not* dinosaurs. Dinosaurs were built to walk and live on land only, although they may have occasionally waded in the water.

Dinosaurs had special skeletal features. Dinosaurs walked differently than other reptiles because of their hips. Dinosaurs had either ornithischian (birdlike) hips or saurischian (lizardlike) hips. Both kinds of hips allowed dinosaurs to walk with their legs tucked under their bodies to support their full weight. This mammal- or birdlike stance is clearly different from the sprawling stance of all living reptiles. A dinosaur would never have dragged its stomach along the

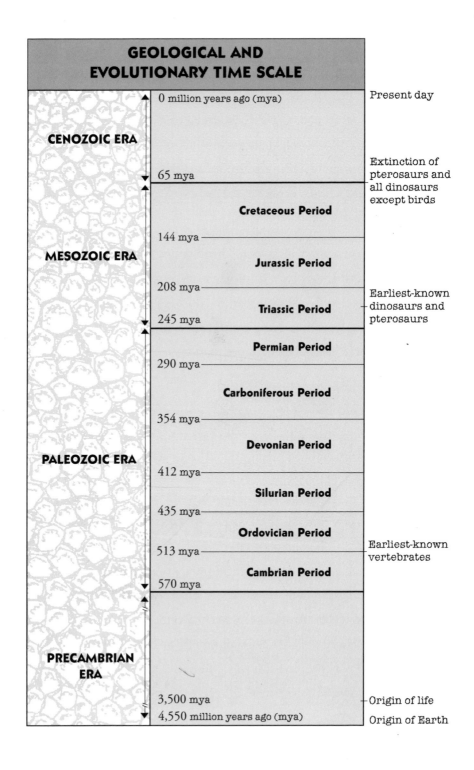

GEOLOGICAL AND EVOLUTIONARY TIME SCALE

CENOZOIC ERA	0 million years ago (mya)	Present day
	65 mya	Extinction of pterosaurs and all dinosaurs except birds
MESOZOIC ERA	Cretaceous Period	
	144 mya	
	Jurassic Period	
	208 mya	Earliest-known dinosaurs and pterosaurs
	Triassic Period	
	245 mya	
PALEOZOIC ERA	Permian Period	
	290 mya	
	Carboniferous Period	
	354 mya	
	Devonian Period	
	412 mya	
	Silurian Period	
	435 mya	
	Ordovician Period	Earliest-known vertebrates
	513 mya	
	Cambrian Period	
	570 mya	
PRECAMBRIAN ERA	3,500 mya	Origin of life
	4,550 million years ago (mya)	Origin of Earth

ground like a crocodile or lizard would. Other distinguishing skeletal features of dinosaurs include:

- Three or more vertebrae (backbones) attaching the spine to the hip.
- A ball-and-socket joint attaching the legs to the hip for increased mobility and flexibility.
- High ankles and long foot bones. (Dinosaurs walked on their toes.)
- A simple hinge joint at the ankle.
- Three or fewer finger bones on the fourth finger of each forefoot (hand) or no fourth finger at all.
- Three to five clawed or hoofed toes on the hind limb (foot).

Understanding Dinosaurs

The study of extinct fossil organisms is called *paleontology*. (*Paleo* means "ancient.") Paleontologists use fossil traces of ancient organisms as a window into life in the distant past, before the evolution of modern man.

Most of what we know about dinosaurs comes from our knowledge of their fossilized skeletons and the layers of Earth in which they are found. Putting a dinosaur together is like doing a jigsaw puzzle without a picture to follow. Fortunately, because dinosaurs were vertebrates, all dinosaur skeletons are similar in some ways. A basic knowledge of vertebrate skeletons, and of dinosaur skeletons in particular, helps guide the paleontologist in putting together a new fossil jigsaw puzzle.

While no human being has ever seen a dinosaur in the flesh, much can be revealed by studying the fossil clues. The paleontologist must have a firm grasp of scientific methods and fact. He or she must also have imagination and a knack for solving mysteries. Fossils provide evidence for the construction of dinosaurs. The paleontologist examines these facts and tries to understand how they affected the lifestyle and behavior of dinosaurs.

Our knowledge of dinosaurs grows every year. This book, and others in the series, will help you understand the many kinds of dinosaurs and how they lived. It is based on the latest scientific evidence and shows us that dinosaur science is alive and well all around the world. After all, if scientific estimates are correct, there may have been as many as 1,200 unique kinds, or genera, of dinosaurs, only about 350 of which have yet been discovered.[1] If you decide to make dinosaur science your life, maybe one day you will add a new dinosaur or two to the list.

The Theropods

Most visitors to dinosaur museums have one thing in common: a fascination with the meat-eating dinosaurs.

When visitors meet the skeleton of *Tyrannosaurus* ("tyrant lizard") for the first time, they are overwhelmed by its enormity. They see the mouthful of banana-sized teeth and the huge talons on its strangely birdlike feet. They note the gigantic head and legs as thick as tree limbs and imagine the steely stare of its cold, hostile eyes. Even its backbone, running from its skull to the tip of its tail, is monstrous, lengthening the creature to 38 feet (11.6 meters). The visitors realize how truly small we humans are when they stand next to the skeleton of *Tyrannosaurus rex* (*T. rex*). If a *Tyrannosaurus* were alive today, it could open its jaws wide enough for a Siberian tiger to jump through. What an amazing circus act that would be, if only it were possible.

When they first set eyes on the skeleton of *Velociraptor* ("swift thief"), they may wonder what all the excitement was about in *Jurassic Park*, because the actual dinosaur is surprisingly small. This creature was no more than 2 feet (0.6 meters) tall at the hip and measured an unimpressive 6 feet (1.8 meters) long. Yet this lightweight, agile predator had powerful legs and a large slashing claw on each foot. It was probably as horrific a killer as ever walked the earth.

Turning another corner in a museum, visitors may see the tiny skeleton of what was the world's smallest dinosaur, *Compsognathus* ("elegant jaw"). It was about the size of a chicken and had tiny teeth and delicate claws on its two-fingered

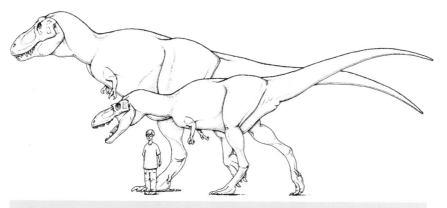

The enormous *Tyrannosaurus* towers over another meat-eating dinosaur, *Gorgosaurus*. They are shown in comparison with an average twelve year old.

hands. It was probably only a monster in the eyes of insects and small lizards.

As spectacularly different as these dinosaurs were, they all had one thing in common. They were all part of the diverse group of dinosaurs known as theropods ("beast foot"). The group includes all the known meat-eating dinosaurs.

Theropod dinosaurs were the stuff of nightmares. They were the monsters of the dinosaur world, the hunters of the gentle plant eaters, the shadow of death lurking in the dangerous forests of the Mesozoic Era. They were the incredibly scary and horrible brutes that kids love so much because they were often big and bad and now, thankfully, are extinct.

Even if *Tyrannosaurus* and its kin were alive today, it is unlikely that they could be tamed. Like other dinosaurs, theropods had relatively small brains compared to today's top predators. They probably reserved their intelligence for the things that mattered most: seeking, killing, and eating prey; and mating.

Diversity of the Theropods

About 40 percent of all the individual kinds, or genera, of dinosaurs recognized so far were theropods.[2] This figure is quite high considering that meat eaters probably made up a much smaller part of the dinosaur population than the plant-eating animals that were their prey.

The reason for this is that when it comes to variety, theropods ruled. They were the only major group of dinosaurs to have spanned the entire age of dinosaurs—all 160 million

Theropods ranged in size from small, chicken-sized creatures to huge creatures, such as *Gigantosaurus*, whose skull is shown here.

years—in one form or another. They were the first dinosaurs ever to walk the earth, feeding on insects and small animals such as lizards. They were also among the last dinosaurs to perish. They lived in every corner of the dinosaur world and evolved into many different kinds of meat eaters, one even leading to modern birds. They ranged in size from the tiniest of dinosaurs, the chicken-sized *Compsognathus*, to hulking monsters such as *Tyrannosaurus*, *Giganotosaurus* ("gigantic southern lizard"), and *Carcharodontosaurus* ("sharp-toothed lizard"). In between these extremes were many varieties of the basic two-legged carnivorous dinosaur.

This book is devoted to the creatures that played the role of villain in the days of the dinosaurs.

CHAPTER 2

ORIGINS AND EVOLUTION

When the first dinosaurs evolved, they were part of a rich biological history that had already spanned hundreds of millions of years.

Dinosaurs descended from land vertebrates. Land vertebrates descended from ocean vertebrates, which began wandering onto land about 370 million years ago. All of these early animals lived at least part of their lives in the water. Even today's amphibians, which take to the land as adults, begin as waterborne creatures. Adult amphibians still need to return to the water to lay their eggs.

The most important biological event leading to true land animals was the evolution of the amniotes, vertebrate animals that could fertilize their eggs internally. These included reptiles and birds, which laid shelled eggs on land, and mammals, whose fertilized eggs developed within their bodies. Humans, birds, lizards, snakes, turtles, and even dinosaurs are all related by being amniotes.

Dinosaurs fall within the group of vertebrates known as Reptilia, or reptiles. Reptiles are egg-laying, backboned animals with scaly skin. The different kinds of reptiles, living and extinct, are grouped by certain features of their skeletons. Most important is the design of the reptilian skull. Dinosaurs fall within the subclass Diapsida, which includes reptiles whose skulls had a pair of openings behind each eye. Diapsida is divided into two groups: the lepidosaurs and the archosaurs. Lepidosaurs consist of the kinds of lizards and snakes that live today. Archosaurs consist of the thecodonts, some of which were small meat eaters that had begun to run on two feet; the crocodiles (living and extinct); the pterosaurs (extinct flying reptiles); and the dinosaurs.[1] All dinosaurs are probably descendants of a single common archosaurian ancestor.[2]

The dinosaurs and other diapsid reptiles were some of the most successful branches of land vertebrates of all time. Dinosaurs first appeared about 225 million years ago and began to spread rapidly by the end of the Triassic Period.[3] Figure 1 summarizes the evolution of vertebrates leading to the dinosaurs and their bird descendants.

Dinosaur Beginnings

The earliest archosaurs were carnivores. Some evolved with four sprawling legs, while others gradually began to walk or sprint for short distances on only two legs. By the Late Triassic Period, about 225 million years ago, some two-legged, meat-eating creatures had evolved specialized hips and legs to help them stand erect. This supported the full weight of their bodies

Vertebrate Origins and Evolution
Leading to Dinosaurs

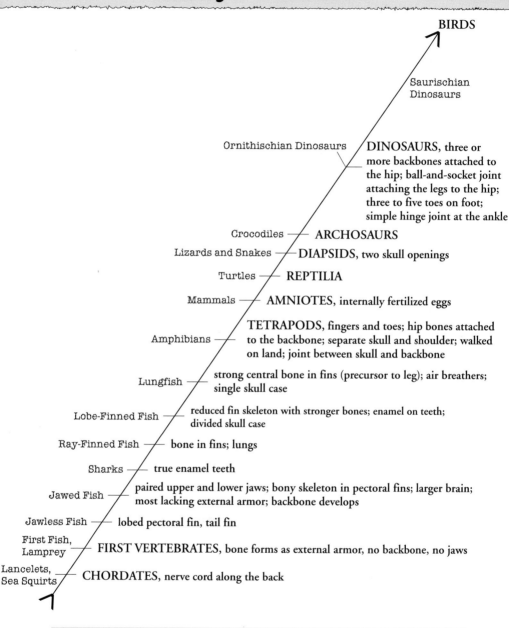

BIRDS

Saurischian
Dinosaurs

Ornithischian Dinosaurs

DINOSAURS, three or
more backbones attached to
the hip; ball-and-socket joint
attaching the legs to the hip;
three to five toes on foot;
simple hinge joint at the ankle

Crocodiles — ARCHOSAURS

Lizards and Snakes — DIAPSIDS, two skull openings

Turtles — REPTILIA

Mammals — AMNIOTES, internally fertilized eggs

TETRAPODS, fingers and toes; hip bones attached
to the backbone; separate skull and shoulder; walked
on land; joint between skull and backbone

Amphibians

strong central bone in fins (precursor to leg); air breathers;
single skull case

Lungfish

reduced fin skeleton with stronger bones; enamel on teeth;
divided skull case

Lobe-Finned Fish

Ray-Finned Fish — bone in fins; lungs

Sharks — true enamel teeth

Jawed Fish

paired upper and lower jaws; bony skeleton in pectoral fins; larger brain;
most lacking external armor; backbone develops

Jawless Fish — lobed pectoral fin, tail fin

First Fish,
Lamprey — FIRST VERTEBRATES, bone forms as external armor, no backbone, no jaws

Lancelets,
Sea Squirts — CHORDATES, nerve cord along the back

Figure 1. This diagram shows how vertebrate animals evolved to yield dinosaurs.
The steps along the way include evolutionary changes that are directly
related to the characteristics of dinosaurs. The time span from the appearance
of the first chordates to the last dinosaur is about 460 million years.

while they walked on two feet. They ranged in size from about 6 inches (15 centimeters) to 13 feet (4 meters). These kinds of archosaurs led to the first dinosaurs.

By the late part of the Triassic Period, two distinct branches of dinosaurs had evolved based on their hip designs. The *saurischians* included the meat-eating theropods and plant-eating sauropods. The *ornithischians* included the remaining assortment of plant eaters, such as ornithopods (duckbills, iguanodonts, and others) and armored and horned dinosaurs.

Theropods were the first dinosaurs to appear and among the last to become extinct during the 160-million-year reign of the dinosaurs. They evolved into many diverse kinds and sizes. They adapted some of the most advanced carnivorous weaponry ever possessed by land-dwelling creatures.

Eoraptor ("dawn thief"), *Herrerasaurus* ("Herrera's lizard"), and *Staurikosaurus* ("cross lizard") are the most primitive known dinosaurs. All have been found in Late Triassic deposits of South America dating from about 225 to 230 million years ago. They resembled small theropods in many ways.[4] From these distinctive beginnings came a remarkable lineage of theropods that menaced every generation of plant-eating dinosaurs until their demise at the end of the Cretaceous Period.

The Theropod Groups

Theropods, which included all meat-eating dinosaurs, came in an astounding variety. Paleontologists study the features of

Theropods include all the meat-eating dinosaurs. The group includes the well-known *Tyrannosaurus*.

their bones and the times when they existed to understand how the different theropods were related.

While some theropods, such as *Allosaurus* ("different lizard"), *Tyrannosaurus*, *Coelophysis* ("hollow form"), and others are quite well known from fossil specimens, most are not. More than 75 percent of the known theropods are

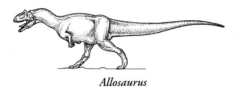

Allosaurus

understood only from the partial remains of single individuals. This leaves many gaps in our theories. Paleontologists do not always agree on which theropods were most closely related to each other. Theories about the genealogy of theropods become more believable every year as more specimens are discovered.

Coelophysis

It is easiest to distinguish between one kind of theropod and another by understanding the different groups to which they belonged. The summary on the next two pages names the theropod groups. They are organized chronologically by known specimens.

Ceratosauroidea—("horned lizards")

Named after one of the earliest members of the group, the large horned theropod *Ceratosaurus*. Also includes some theropods from the Southern Hemisphere, from South America, Madagascar, and India. They are often adorned with thick brows, horns, or other bony structures on the skull.

Time: Late Jurassic to Late Cretaceous.

Abelisaurus, Carnotaurus, Elaphrosaurus, Indosuchus, Majungatholus

Ceratosaurus

Coelophysoidea—("hollow forms")

Early, mostly small theropods with grasping hands, long arms, flexible necks, and long, low skulls. Some larger forms have skull crests.

Time: Late Triassic to Early Jurassic.

Dilophosaurus, Liliensternus, Syntarsus

Coelophysis

Spinosauroidea—("thorn lizards")

Large predators with an elongated jaw resembling that of a crocodile, long hand claws, and a large spine or sail running along the back.

Time: Middle Jurassic to Late Cretaceous.

Baryonyx, Spinosaurus, Torvosaurus

Suchomimus

Allosauroidea—("different lizards")

Large predators with strong, three-clawed arms, powerful neck, and lightly built head.

Time: Early Jurassic to Late Cretaceous.

Acrocanthosaurus, Cryolophosaurus, Szechuanosaurus

Allosaurus

Compsognathidae—("elegant jaw")

Small, lightly built theropod with similarities to *Archaeopteryx*, the first bird. Distantly related to tyrannosaurs.

Time: Late Jurassic.

Compsognathus

Troodontidae—("wounding teeth")

Person-sized predators with big brains, big eyes, long arms, and long necks. They also had a retractable claw on the second toe, but it was not as strong or as large as those of the dromaeosaurs.

Time: Late Jurassic to Late Cretaceous.

Saurornithoides, Troodon

THEROPOD FAMILIES	SOME MEMBERS

Ornithomimoidea—("bird mimics")

Speedy ostrichlike theropods with long legs and toothless beaks.

Time: Early to Late Cretaceous.

Alvarezsaurus, Gallimimus, Struthiomimus

Ornithomimus

Dromaeosauridae—("running lizards")

Agile, sickle-clawed theropods ranging from small to medium size. They may have attacked while leaping, using the claws on their second toes to slash at prey.

Time: Early to Late Cretaceous.

Dromaeosaurus, Utahraptor, Velociraptor

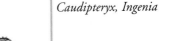

Deinonychus

Oviraptorosauria—("egg thieves")

Small birdlike theropods with strong arms, long hand claws, and a short but deep skull with a nasal bump, a toothless beak, and two small pointed teeth in the roof of its mouth. Earliest members included feathered theropods.

Time: Early to Late Cretaceous.

Caudipteryx, Ingenia

Oviraptor

Therizinosauridea—("scythe lizards")

Mysterious, poorly known group of theropods with elongated hand claws, robust limbs, and often large bodies. At least one specimen appears to have had feathers (*Beipiaosaurus*).

Time: Early to Late Cretaceous.

Beipiaosaurus, Therizinosaurus

Tyrannosauridae—("tyrant lizards")

Some of the largest theropods, sporting huge heads, long robust teeth, powerful legs, and short two-clawed hands.

Time: Late Cretaceous.

Albertosaurus, Tarbosaurus

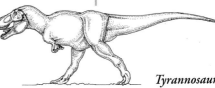

Tyrannosaurus

Aves—(birds)

Modern descendants of non-avian dinosaurs, probably the dromaeosaurs.

All modern birds.

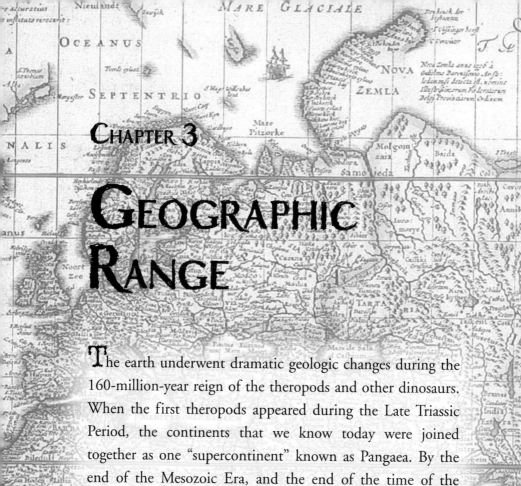

CHAPTER 3

GEOGRAPHIC RANGE

The earth underwent dramatic geologic changes during the 160-million-year reign of the theropods and other dinosaurs. When the first theropods appeared during the Late Triassic Period, the continents that we know today were joined together as one "supercontinent" known as Pangaea. By the end of the Mesozoic Era, and the end of the time of the dinosaurs, the continents had broken apart and formed the major landmasses known today as North and South America, Africa, Europe, Asia, Australia, and Antarctica.

When the continents were joined, it was possible for dinosaurs to travel across the dry land. The theropods and prosauropods, the earliest known dinosaurs, spread rapidly around the globe while the continents were still connected. This accounts for similarities of some of the earliest theropods found in North and South America. By the Middle Jurassic Period, Pangaea had begun to split apart, first dividing into two landmasses. The northern landmass was called Laurasia and included the areas that we now know as North America, Europe, and Asia. The southern landmass was called Gondwana and included the regions now known as South America, Africa, India, Australia, and Antarctica.

As the continents continued to separate, it was harder for the dinosaurs to spread to different areas. Today's arrangement of the continents was formed by the end of the Cretaceous Period, the end of the dinosaur era.

Theropods were perhaps the most widespread of all the dinosaurs. Their remains have been discovered on every continent, in such far-flung places as northern Alaska and Antarctica.

The greatest concentrations of theropods have been found in the northwestern mountain states of North

TRIASSIC

EARLY JURASSIC

EARLY CRETACEOUS

Range of Theropod Fossil Locations Around the World

America, western Canada, western Europe, central Asia, and China. New frontiers of theropod research may bring new and different specimens to light in Argentina, Africa, and as yet unexplored areas in China and Mongolia.

Chapter 4

Anatomy

All organisms are made up of biological structures, such as the skeleton. The study of these structures is called anatomy. Studying the anatomy of an organism is distinct from studying how the structures are *used* by the organism, which is called physiology and is covered in the next chapter.

Dinosaurs Are Vertebrates

Dinosaurs are part of the group of animals known as vertebrates—animals with backbones. The first vertebrates were fish, followed by amphibians, reptiles, dinosaurs, and mammals and birds. The first vertebrates appeared about 520 million years ago in the form of jawless fish.[1] Dinosaurs first walked the earth about 225 million years ago, nearly 300 million years after fish had begun to populate the oceans.

Regardless of whether they live in water, walk on land, or fly in the air, all vertebrates share some common characteristics. The most basic common feature of the vertebrate body is that one side of the body is a mirror image of the other. This principle is called bilateral symmetry.

A second common feature is that the organs of vertebrates have descended from what were basically the same organs in their ancestors. This idea is called the principle of homology.

Dinosaurs shared many similar skeletal features with other vertebrates, living and extinct. Even though we rarely, if ever, see the actual remains of soft tissue or organs of the dinosaurs—such as the brain, heart, lungs, liver, and gut—we can assume that they shared many of the internal organs of today's land-dwelling vertebrates. These ideas allow scientists to speculate about what a living dinosaur was really like.

The Dinosaur Hip

All dinosaurs are divided into two large groups based on the structure of their hipbones. The saurischian ("lizard-hipped") group is comprised of the two-legged, meat-eating theropods; the four-legged, long-necked, plant-eating sauropods; and the two-legged, plant-eating prosauropods. The ornithischian ("bird-hipped") group includes all others, such as armored, horned, and duck-billed dinosaurs.

Both kinds of dinosaur hips allowed the hind legs to be attached underneath the body so that they could bear the entire weight of the creature. The hind legs were also connected to the hip with a ball-and-socket joint. This provided dinosaurs with increased flexibility and mobility over their reptile ancestors. The front legs were positioned underneath the body to help bear the weight of those dinosaurs that walked on all fours.

The legs of a modern reptile, such as a crocodile or lizard, are attached at the sides of their body and do not support the full weight of their body while the creature is at rest. Reptiles lay their bellies on the ground and rise up only when they need to move. On the other hand, the position of a dinosaur was "always up." Dinosaurs must have been more active and energetic than today's reptiles simply because it requires more stamina to hold up the weight of the body as they did.

Dinosaur legs were designed more like those of mammals or birds but with some clear distinctions. While the joints in their shoulders and hips had much flexibility, those in the knees and elbows did not. This, combined with an ankle that was more like a door hinge than a ball and socket, restricted the bending of a dinosaur's forelimbs and hind limbs in one plane of motion, forward and backward. Unlike humans and other mammals, who can move sideways with ease, a dinosaur had to turn its body if it wanted to move to the side. Dinosaurs would have made lousy soccer goalies.

The Theropod Body

Theropods of all sizes were designed for one thing: to kill and devour other creatures. Scientists know this from studying their bones and the clues that reveal their predatory nature.

As carnivores, theropod dinosaurs had the same needs as other meat-eating creatures. They needed to run faster than their prey. They needed weapons of some sort for rapidly inflicting wounds on their victims. They also required specialized teeth for grasping and ripping off chunks of flesh. Their senses of vision, smell, and hearing may have been highly acute to help them locate and track their prey.[2] In these ways, theropod dinosaurs were no different from other meat-eating animals that came before and after them. Even today's top predators, such as the lion, tiger, and crocodile, share these same basic needs. But during the many millions of years that they evolved, theropod dinosaurs apparently became some of the most sophisticated predators the world has ever seen.

In addition to the saurischian hip, which gave theropods a powerful upright posture, several other unique physical characteristics made them excellent predators, as the following list will show.

- They walked on two legs (bipedal). Most theropods had long legs, making them faster than most of their prey. The dromaeosaurs—a group of meat eaters such as *Velociraptor* with a sickle claw on each foot—were an exception. They may not have been able to outrun all of their prey, because their legs were short.

- They had large openings in their skulls, reducing the weight of the head.

- Their limb bones were hollow, making them lightweight.

- Most had sharp, curved, serrated teeth. The teeth were curved toward the back of the mouth and would pull the prey farther into the mouth with each bite. They would also prevent the prey from squirming back out.

- They had large, sharp, curved, pointed claws on the hands and sometimes the feet. Claws on the hands were used to seize and tear the guts out of their prey.

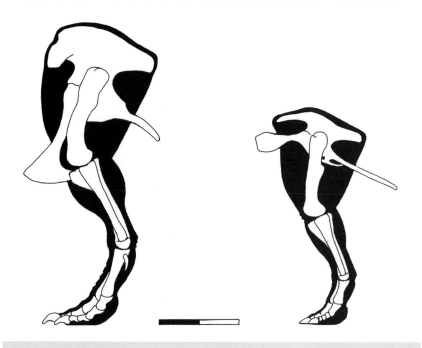

The longer legs of *Tyrannosaurus* (left) helped it run faster than other dinosaurs, such as *Edmontosaurus* (right). (Scale bar = 3 feet, or 1 meter)

Some dromaeosaurs, or raptors, had oversized claws on the second toe of each foot that could also be used to slash and wound.

- Their four-clawed feet had three large toes to support their weight and one small outside toe that was not large enough to stand on. They had good balance and their claws helped maintain a firm grip as they moved.

- Most theropods had long tails. These were often stiffened so that they did not bend down or touch the ground while the creature was standing or walking. The tail probably helped these dinosaurs maintain excellent balance.

- Theropods had larger brains than most other dinosaurs. They also had well-developed nerve centers for the senses of sight, smell, and hearing. Some had forward-looking eyes, giving them stereoscopic vision. This meant that they could see the same thing with both eyes at the same time, like people, lions, and other predators. Stereoscopic vision gives predators good depth perception. With this, they can locate their prey more precisely, which is important when chasing and grabbing prey on the run. Smell and hearing are also important to carnivorous beasts. (See "Senses" on page 49 for additional detail.)

- The strong, muscular necks and heads gave them flexibility and strength when attacking and biting.

Theropod Skulls and Teeth

The head of a large theropod dinosaur must have been a scary sight indeed. The large eyes for locating prey and a gaping mouth full of sharp teeth must have been the last thing to be seen by many a plant eater.

Theropod skulls ranged in size from petite—only 3 inches (7.6 centimeters) long—to mammoth—about 6 feet (1.8 meters) long.

Most were equipped with an impressive array of sharp, serrated teeth for chomping meat, although a few were toothless. Theropods without teeth had bony beaks and probably ate small prey such as insects, small mammals, lizards, and possibly plants.

Predatory dinosaurs with teeth had only one kind of tooth in their mouths—the sharp, serrated teeth for slicing and tearing flesh. They had no flat teeth for grinding and

Allosaurus Skeleton

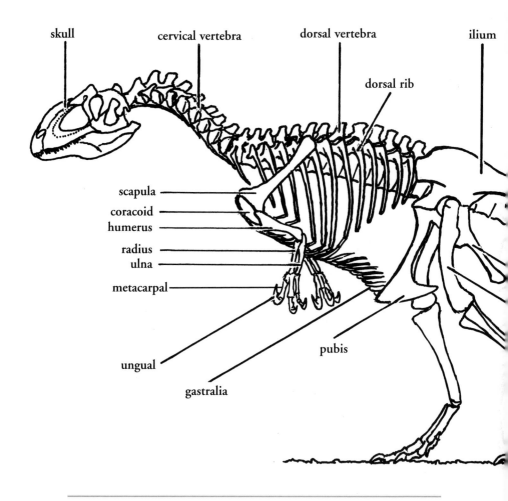

skull

cervical vertebra

dorsal vertebra

ilium

dorsal rib

scapula

coracoid

humerus

radius

ulna

metacarpal

ungual

pubis

gastralia

chewing. But even the sharp teeth came in several sizes and varieties.

The individual serrations on the teeth, called denticles, served the same function as the jagged peaks on the edge of a steak knife. The denticles were closely spaced and were separated by slots that enabled the teeth to grip and tear meat fibers more easily. Dinosaurs continually lost and regrew teeth throughout their lives, which explains why many specimens have teeth of different sizes. Some teeth were still growing back at the time of the dinosaur's death.

The teeth of large predatory dinosaurs were strong. They were probably the primary killing weapon in large theropods such as *Tyrannosaurus, Allosaurus,* and *Carcharodontosaurus.*

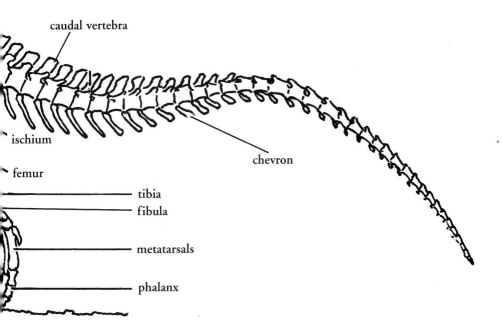

caudal vertebra

ischium

chevron

femur

tibia

fibula

metatarsals

phalanx

The largest of these teeth were positioned more along the sides of the jaw than the front, where they could be most effective in cutting bones and flesh.

Small theropods usually had weapons other than their teeth, including claws on their hands and feet. As a result, the teeth of these dinosaurs were not as big or as strong as those of their larger cousins. However, smaller meat eaters had more teeth. The 7-foot- (2.1-meter-) long *Troodon* had about 122 teeth, whereas the 38-foot- (11.6 -meter-) long *Tyrannosaurus* had about 60.[3]

The joint between the neck and skull was highly flexible in theropods. It allowed them to turn their heads from side to side with ease. Flexible skull and jaw joints could absorb the physical shock caused by the vicious biting and dismembering of prey with the teeth. Some theropod jaws, such as that of *Allosaurus*, may have been able to flex wider to permit the swallowing of overly large morsels of meat.

Anatomy of the *Tyrannosaurus* Skull. Skulls are composed of many small parts. Each part has its own name. Most of these parts are found in all theropod skulls, but they vary in size and shape depending on the particular kind of dinosaur. Dinosaur skulls are often found in fragments, so paleontologists must be able to recognize dinosaur types from the smallest of pieces. The elements found in theropod skulls are illustrated on the next page using *Tyrannosaurus*, the most famous theropod.

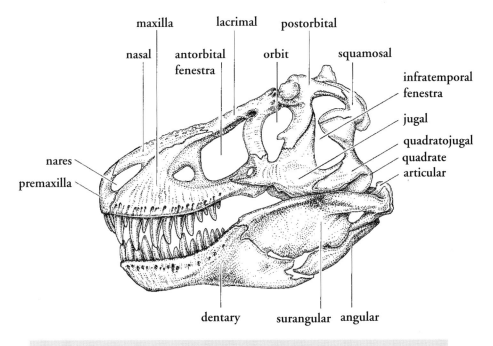

Tyrannosaurus skull

Dinosaur Skin

Dinosaur skin, like other soft body parts of these animals, was almost never fossilized. The skin of dinosaurs easily decomposed and disappeared long before fossilization could take place. Although there is some evidence about what dinosaur skin looked like, it is extremely rare, especially for theropods.

Dinosaur skin impressions are the only clear evidence we have for what dinosaurs might have looked like on the outside. Artists who specialize in the reproduction of dinosaurs

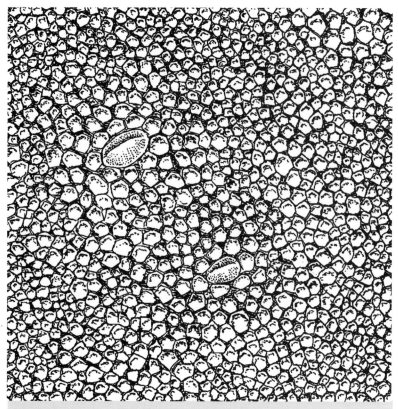

The skin pattern shown here is based on fossil skin impressions of the theropod *Carnotaurus*.

are particularly interested in skin impressions so that they can make their drawings accurate.

All of the evidence uncovered so far regarding dinosaur skin shows that they had nonoverlapping scales similar to those of the modern monitor lizard. These scales varied in size across different parts of the body. They were generally smaller, for flexibility, around the head and joints such as the neck and knees and larger along broad parts of the body and tail.

There are two sources of evidence for dinosaur skin: fossilized skin impressions and dinosaur mummies.

Fossilized skin impressions. A fossilized skin impression is not the dinosaur skin itself, but the pattern of the skin that was left in the mud where a dinosaur died. Skin impressions can often be associated with a specific kind of dinosaur if the fossilized bones are found nearby. Like trackways—the fossilized footprints of dinosaurs—skin impressions are known as trace fossils. They represent a trace of the dinosaur that made them, rather than being fossilized parts of the dinosaur

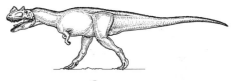

Ceratosaurus

itself. A number of good skin impressions have been found for plant-eating dinosaurs, particularly the hadrosaurs. But there is little evidence for the skin patterns of theropods. Evidence from *Ceratosaurus* ("horned lizard"), *Tyrannosaurus*, and *Carnotaurus* ("meat-eating bull") all show the typical scaly skin.

Dinosaur mummies. There are some extremely rare conditions under which a dinosaur carcass may have been preserved with fossilized skin intact. In these cases, the body of the dinosaur probably dried, undisturbed by scavengers, in the hot sun before being buried. The skin of the creature therefore became stretched tight over its bones, and even though the skin itself eventually disintegrated, the process of fossilization preserved its pattern throughout the specimen. There are no known cases of this kind of preservation for theropods.

The most famous dinosaur mummy is that of a duck-billed dinosaur on display at the American Museum of Natural History in New York.

Skin color is never preserved in skin impressions or fossils. However, scientists can guess that the colors of dinosaurs varied, as color does in today's reptiles and birds. Some dinosaurs, especially the smaller ones, may have had camouflaging colors to help them blend in with their surroundings. Color may have also been a way to tell the difference between males and females of the species, and therefore may have been a means for attracting a mate.

CHAPTER 5

PHYSIOLOGY

Physiology is the study of how a body operates. The physiology of theropods is understood by comparing the evidence from fossils to the anatomy and physiology of today's creatures. Other physical evidence, such as trackways, has also been used to piece together what we know about theropods and other dinosaurs.

Brains and Smarts

Some of the smaller theropods were the Einsteins of dinosaurs. To understand how this can be known, one needs to know how the size of the brain can be used to measure an animal's "smarts."

How smart were dinosaurs? The question is not easy to answer. After all, what *is* intelligence? Intelligence might be described as the ability to process information, or to learn. Since this is something we will never be able to observe in dinosaurs, we must rely on other clues to intelligence that are found in the fossil record. Chief among these is the size of a dinosaur's brain in comparison to the size of its body.

In examining many kinds of living animals, scientists have found a relationship between intelligence and the size of the brain compared to the size of the creature's body. A species whose brain is larger than expected for its body size is usually more intelligent. This evidence allows scientists to compare the intelligence of animals of different body sizes, say a Pekingese dog with an Irish wolfhound. By this measure, mammals and birds are considered to be more intelligent than fish, amphibians, and reptiles. What makes humans so unusual is that our brain size is seven times greater than should be expected for a creature with our body size.

The brain, like other soft tissues and organs, has not been preserved in the fossil record. However, the approximate size of a dinosaur's brain can be determined by measuring and casting the cavity in the skull where the brain once was. This cavity is called the braincase. Unfortunately, most dinosaur skull material is incomplete and does not include the brain-case. Even when the braincase is present, the space is often not well preserved due to the compression and crushing of the skull during fossilization. Measurements have thus far been made for less than 5 percent of all known dinosaurs. Much work remains in this area.[1]

Compared to other dinosaurs, theropods had higher ratios of brain weight to body weight. That is why they are considered the brainiest of dinosaurs. Small theropods, such as *Troodon*, had the largest brains in comparison to body weight.[2] This made them comparable to some modern birds and mammals. Many other dinosaurs, though maybe not as gifted, are still comparable to modern crocodilians and reptiles when it comes to the size of their brain compared to body weight.[3]

Senses

Predatory creatures rely on their senses to find their prey. An animal with a good sense of smell might pick up the scent of a prey animal long before it is in sight. It might also detect the odor of blood or decaying flesh. A good sense of hearing, like smell, provides clues to the presence of prey before it can be seen. Keen eyesight is important for pinpointing and running down the prey once it has been located.

All of these senses were certainly important to predatory dinosaurs. The strength of these senses in dinosaurs can be guessed by studying the braincase and other parts of the skull.

Holes in the Head. The braincase, or brain cavity, in a dinosaur skull held the brain and the many connections between the brain and other parts of the body. Nerves connected the brain to other organs through holes in the braincase.

The brains of modern vertebrates—particularly of reptiles and birds—are similar in many ways. The sense of smell is located at the front of the brain in the olfactory lobe, and vision is concentrated in an optic lobe near the center. Observing the kinds of nerve connections that exist in today's animals can help a paleontologist identify the locations of similar features in skulls. The parts of the brain used for vision and smell appear to have been highly developed in theropod dinosaurs.[4]

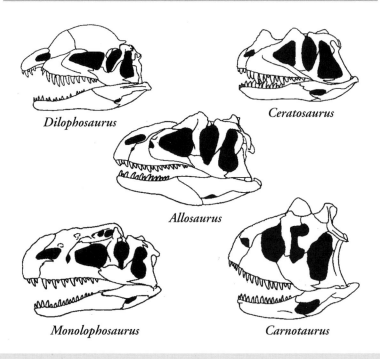

Dilophosaurus

Ceratosaurus

Allosaurus

Monolophosaurus

Carnotaurus

Theropod skulls of all sizes had many openings, making them relatively lightweight. The brain was located inside the top rear of the skull.

Vision. The eyes of theropods were larger than those of other kinds of dinosaurs of similar size. They are especially large in the smaller, big-brained theropods such as *Troodon*. Scientists know that theropods had large eyes based on the size of the eye sockets in the skull. Sometimes the thin, bony eye rings that encircled the outer edge of the eyeball are present in the fossil. The same kinds of rings are seen today in birds and some reptiles.

While most meat eaters had eyes that could look only to the sides, like those of a lizard, many of the latter theropods, including *Tyrannosaurus* and *Troodon*, had eyes that were more forward-looking. This provided an overlapping, stereoscopic field of vision.[5] It made it easier for these dinosaurs to judge the distance to a prey animal trying to evade them.

Hearing. Like the brain cavity seen in dinosaur skulls, pockets in the skull once held the parts of the dinosaur ear. Ear bones are sometimes found in dinosaur skulls. Based on these ear bones, scientists believe that most dinosaurs, whether predator or prey, probably had good hearing.

Certain meat eaters had special adaptations for hearing. *Troodon* and other similar predators had a large, complicated inner ear that probably helped them accurately detect the source of a sound. It may have also allowed them to detect low-frequency sounds more readily, like the distant footfall of a large plant eater or even the low bellows of a duckbill communicating with its herd.[6]

Smell. The braincase of theropod dinosaurs shows that they had an excellent sense of smell. However, there was not much supporting evidence for this from other parts of the skull until recently.

The smelling power of *Nannotyrannus* ("small tyrant"), which some paleontologists believe is a young *Tyrannosaurus*, seems to have been enhanced by a filter of thin, bony plates and membranes behind the nose opening. Something similar to this is seen in mammals and improves the ability to smell and to capture moisture from the air. Now that this has been found in *Nannotyrannus*, paleontologists are looking for similar structures in other dinosaurs.

Computerized tomography, or CT scanning, provides paleontologists with a marvelous new way of examining dinosaur skulls without physically damaging them. The Field Museum of Natural History in Chicago has been doing extensive CT work on the skull of one of the most complete *Tyrannosaurus* skeletons ever found. Nicknamed "Sue" after Sue Hendrickson, the field paleontologist who found it, this hefty tyrannosaur is giving new meaning to the saying "follow your nose." It appears that the bundle of nerves connecting *Tyrannosaurus'* brain to its nose were much larger than ever thought. The hole in the braincase through which these nerves passed was about the diameter of a peach. By comparison, a smaller hole in the back of the braincase, where the brain connected to the spinal cord, is closer to the size of a grape. This suggests that *Tyrannosaurus* and its relatives were adapted to make extensive use of their sense of smell.[7]

Growth Rate

Newly hatched dinosaurs were small, yet they sometimes grew to enormous sizes—anywhere from ten times to thousands of times their original weight. What can the fossil record tell us about how fast the dinosaurs grew from hatchling to adult?

To understand how fast dinosaurs grew, scientists need three things. The first is a keen knowledge of how fast modern reptiles, birds, and other animals grow. Then they can keep their guesses about dinosaurs in perspective. Information about reptile growth is abundant. Also, reptiles continue to grow throughout their lives, unlike birds and mammals, which

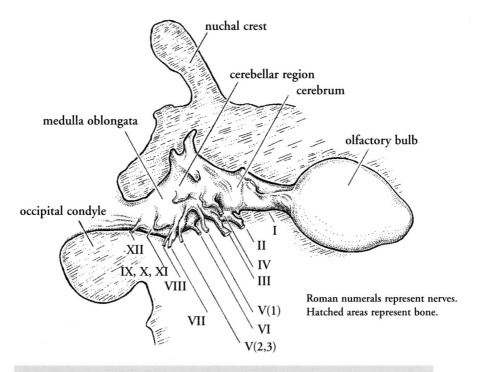

nuchal crest

cerebellar region

cerebrum

medulla oblongata

olfactory bulb

occipital condyle

XII

IX, X, XI

VIII

I

II

IV

III

VII

V(1)

VI

V(2,3)

Roman numerals represent nerves.
Hatched areas represent bone.

The brain of *Tyrannosaurus* and other dinosaurs had the same kinds of nerve connections as modern vertebrates. This allows scientists to understand which parts of the brain were dedicated to which senses.

reach a peak size soon after reaching sexual maturity. Scientists would like to find out which of these patterns of growth applied to dinosaurs.

The second thing needed to understand the growth rates of dinosaurs is a series of fossil skeletons for a given kind of dinosaur that represents several life stages of the dinosaur. This is available in only a few cases for the theropods, including *Syntarsus* ("fused ankle") and *Troodon*.

The third thing needed to understand how fast a dinosaur

grew is a way to connect what is seen in the bones to the growth span of a dinosaur. One attempt to do this uses microscopic studies of dinosaur bone. A magnified cross section of bone can reveal clues about dinosaur growth.

At one extreme, some bones formed in a smooth, continuous pattern. This indicates that the dinosaur was growing continuously and rapidly. At the other extreme, some bone tissue formed in curious rings called lines of arrested growth. These growth rings are much like the seasonal rings in cross sections of trees. This phenomenon is also seen in the bones of modern reptiles. It represents an annual period when growth slows down, perhaps during a cool season when the animal is less active for an extended period.

Some dinosaurs have both kinds of bone tissue. This means that dinosaurs grew at different rates at different times in their lives. It appears that they grew rapidly until they reached adult size, then they slowed down but still continued growing.

Based on the study of growth rings in theropod bone samples, it appears that smaller predatory dinosaurs grew somewhat slowly. *Syntarsus*, a 10-foot (3-meter) Late Triassic meat eater from Zimbabwe, probably approached adult size in about seven years.[8] A later small theropod, *Troodon* from the northwestern United States and western Canada, was most likely fully grown after about five years.[9] These dinosaurs also grew faster at first but slowed down as they neared full growth. Growing up fast would have made them large enough to catch prey at a young age. These rates are faster than those of the modern crocodile but not as rapid as those of birds.

While microscopic bone studies provide some truly intriguing information about possible dinosaur growth rates, they also lead to additional questions. Counting growth rings in bones like those in a tree is not as reliable as originally thought. Different bones in the same dinosaur skeleton sometimes have different numbers of growth rings.

How fast did *Tyrannosaurus* grow? Unfortunately, there is no evidence to help us answer this question. Very few hatchlings and juvenile individuals of the largest meat eaters have been found so far.

Aside from how fast the theropods grew, can paleontologists tell how long an individual may have lived? This question is also tricky. A dinosaur could have lived many more years after its bone stopped producing growth rings. Best guesses for the life span of a dinosaur come from observing modern-day animals with similar sizes and metabolisms. Based on these observations, it is possible that small theropods lived for between fifteen and twenty years, and that larger carnivores lived for more than fifty.

Were Dinosaurs Warm-Blooded?

Scientists think that dinosaurs were not the slow and sluggish creatures that they once thought them to be. Dinosaurs were built for action and could probably have moved quite fast when needed. Some dinosaurs also grew rapidly, outpacing the growth rate often seen in modern mammals. But not all dinosaurs were alike in this way. Some grew quite slowly, and there were many others in between.

Does this tell us whether dinosaurs were endotherms (warm-blooded) or ectotherms (cold-blooded)? This is a question that many paleontologists have argued. Unfortunately, there is no simple answer or single piece of fossil evidence that can tell us for sure.

There are two factors that determine whether an animal is warm- or cold-blooded. One is the source of heat. Was it internal, as in endotherms, or external, as in ectotherms? The other factor is the consistency of body temperature. Was it constant or variable?

If we look at today's animals, we can see that small and large mammals are warm-blooded and that reptiles of all sizes are cold-blooded. Dinosaurs were clearly evolved from reptiles, so they were originally thought to be cold-blooded. However, current thinking shows dinosaurs were highly active and unique kinds of creatures, clearly different from other reptiles in many ways. How could they be so active *and* be cold-blooded?

The answer lies in the huge size of dinosaurs. There are no creatures quite like them alive today. But there is evidence that being cold-blooded does not rule out that a creature can be active and energetic and maintain a constant body temperature. Instead of obtaining most of its body heat from its own internal metabolism, as with warm-blooded animals, a cold-blooded creature may use a method called gigantothermy to maintain its temperature.

Gigantothermy relies on a combination of biologic and environmental factors to work:[10]

A warm, temperate, or subtropical climate, such as that enjoyed by the dinosaurs—Heat absorbed during the day would be retained for many hours past dark in a large dinosaur.[11]

Large body size—The larger the body, the more likely that it would retain heat that was absorbed from the environment or produced internally through normal metabolic processes.

Layers of body insulation—Layers of fat were probably capable of retaining body heat.

A digestive process producing heat—Theropods digested their food using a gastric fermentation process that naturally produced heat as a by-product. The mere volume of the gut of dinosaurs suggests that a lot of heat was generated this way.

Special adaptations of the circulatory system—Blood flow and the circulatory path is used to pass heat from the core or gut of the dinosaur to its surface, where it can be safely shed to avoid overheating. The extensive surface area of the body, including their long tails, may have been part of the strategy for shedding excess heat.

All of the above reasons made it possible for theropods and other forms of large dinosaurs to maintain high body temperatures while still having lower cold-blooded metabolic rates. This could have made a significant difference in the survival of the theropods because a lower metabolism required them to eat less than if they had been endotherms.

The larger the body of a theropod, the more likely it would be able to retain its body heat. Here, a *Tyrannosaurus* rests beneath a tree.

This would allow the theropod population to survive with lower food requirements.

But the theory of gigantothermy comes with a significant problem. It does not account for the metabolic process of a dinosaur while it was young and growing, before it reached a size at which gigantothermy could take over. This remains one of the puzzles of dinosaur metabolism. Perhaps the warm environment was enough to keep them active. This, plus the fact that they were eating more as they grew, might account for their maintaining a constant body temperature without the benefit of gigantothermy.

The smaller theropods such as *Velociraptor* and *Deinonychus* were most likely active creatures with warmer metabolisms.[12] Larger theropods, such as *Allosaurus* and *Tyrannosaurus*, prob-ably had higher metabolic rates as they grew and relied on gigantothermy to maintain internal body heat after becoming fully grown.[13]

Deinonychus

Theropod Speed

How fast could theropods run? You may think there could be no way of knowing. After all, no one has been able to set a dinosaur loose on a racetrack and time it with a stopwatch. But there are ways that paleontologists have tried to answer this question.

Fossil footprints, or trackways, left by dinosaurs are the best clues to the speed of dinosaurs. It is not always easy to identify the maker of the tracks. But theropods, with their three birdlike talons, are easily distinguishable from herbivorous dinosaurs. Most trackways are not long, and they almost always show an animal walking rather than running. However, there is some trackway evidence for running theropods that has been studied to determine their speed.

Having the trackways is not enough, however. A stopwatch is not going to do any good, either. To understand dinosaur speed from trackways, scientists use the length of the strides, the leg length of the dinosaur from the ground to the

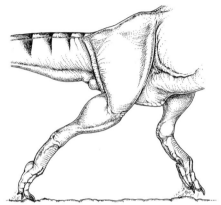

The feet of *Daspletosaurus* (top left) and *Velociraptor* (bottom right) show that these animals ran on their weight-supporting toes.

hip, and a mathematical formula to calculate the speed. A scientist named Robert McNeill Alexander worked out a formula to calculate speed from trackways that is widely used today.[14]

Alexander applied his formula to several kinds of theropod trackways. The top theropod speed he calculated from the trackways of a small theropod, probably of the ostrich-dinosaur variety, was 27 miles per hour (44 kilometers per hour). This is faster than a human can run, somewhat slower than a racehorse, and about the same as a galloping antelope.[15]

Trackways for large running theropods are scarce, and none have been found for a creature the size of *Tyrannosaurus*. Educated guesses are all that can be made about these largest theropods.

Paleontologists Greg Paul and Robert Bakker believe that tyrannosaurs and the ornithomimosaurs ("bird-mimic lizards") were fast runners. This would be possible because of their long limbs, powerful thigh and calf muscles, spring-action knees and ankles, and long, narrow, three-toed feet. Paul suggests that *Tyrannosaurus* as well as the smaller theropods may have normally had a top speed of 45 miles per hour (73 kilometers per hour), and 30 miles per hour (48 kilometers per hour) may have been their absolute minimum for a top speed.[16]

Most other paleontologists, however, are not as convinced about fast-running theropods. Much of this is due to uncertainty over the metabolic rate of the large theropods. John Ostrom, who discovered *Deinonychus* ("terrible claw"), believes that smaller theropods had a high metabolism and could run fast. But he does not agree about *Tyrannosaurus*. He thinks that a top speed for *Tyrannosaurus* of 45 miles per hour was unlikely except for a short period of time, such as a quick burst of energy to lunge or pursue its prey.[17] Others, including James O. Farlow, question whether a large theropod such as *Tyrannosaurus* would risk serious injury by running so fast. By one calculation, *T. rex* would have died if it fell while running at such a high speed.[18]

Males and Females

Telling the males from the females is not easy from skeletons. Paleontologists approach this topic only when an abundance of skeletons from the same kind of dinosaur can be compared. They look for differences that could distinguish the males from the females. Yet, even then, opinions can differ.

Syntarsus and *Coelophysis* are two small theropods that are similar in many ways. Each has been found in a bed of bones that included specimens of many individual adults. In each case, the paleontologist noticed that the

Coelophysis

adults seemed to have come in two basic forms. One was more strongly built and had such features as a larger skull, longer neck, more muscle scars around the elbow and hip, and stronger limbs. But scientists do not always agree on how to tell the males from the females. In the case of *Coelophysis*, the scientist concluded that the larger, stronger individuals were males. In the case of *Syntarsus*, another scientist proposed just the opposite: that the females were the stronger individuals, a variation that can be observed in modern predatory birds.[19]

Differences have also been noticed in specimens of *Tyrannosaurus*. *T. rex* seems to come in two versions, one being more slender and slightly smaller than the other. Like the case of *Syntarsus*, it has been suggested that the larger specimens of *T. rex* are female. The key to this conclusion involves egg laying. In the larger *T. rex* specimens, the back end of the hipbone is more downward pointing, providing a more ample path for the passage of eggs during egg laying.[20] This same anatomical clue has been observed in modern crocodiles.

CHAPTER 6

EGGS AND BABIES

Dinosaurs, like their bird descendants and all known reptiles, hatched from eggs. Dinosaur eggs have been found on every continent but Antarctica and Australia. More than 220 egg sites have been discovered, and three quarters of these are from North America and Asia.[1] Most that have been found date from the Late Cretaceous Period and are from areas that were once relatively dry or semiarid for all or part of the year.

Dinosaur egg nests discovered in the Gobi Desert of Mongolia were buried by sudden sandstorms, dooming many dinosaurs along with their unhatched young.[2] Other nesting sites in the world, such as those in France, India, and northwestern North America, met similar fates in the wake of sandstorms, mud slides, and other rapidly occurring natural catastrophes.

Dinosaur eggs come in various shapes and sizes, including round, oval, and elongated oval varieties.[3] The smallest known dinosaur eggs are round and only about 3 inches (7.6 centimeters) in diameter. The largest, found in China, are elongate and about 18 inches (46 centimeters) long.

Linking a Dinosaur to an Egg

The only way to tell for sure whether an unhatched fossil egg belongs to a certain kind of dinosaur is to find identifiable bones inside. Some remarkable discoveries in recent years have greatly increased our knowledge of which dinosaurs laid which kinds of eggs. Although the bones of unhatched dinosaurs are delicate and small, some identifying features such as the shape of the skull allow scientists to clearly identify which dinosaur is inside the egg.

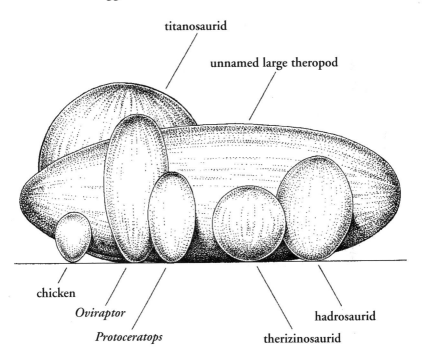

Shapes of various kinds of eggs including those of sauropod dinosaurs, a chicken, the horned dinosaur *Protoceratops*, *Oviraptor*, and a therizinosaur dinosaur (shown to scale).

Elongated eggs are now associated with theropod dinosaurs. Eggs of a troodontid found in China are small, measuring only about 6 inches (15 centimeters) long. Similar eggs have been found in Montana and are attributed to *Troodon*.

The largest known eggs are not from the largest known dinosaurs, as one might expect. They are from a theropod group called the therizinosaurs. Their eggs measure up to a whopping 18.5 inches (47 centimeters) long. They have been positively identified based on the skeleton of an embryo found inside one of these eggs. They were discovered in Xixia, China, as part of a nest containing twenty-six such eggs.[4]

Egg-Laying Patterns

A nest of eggs is called a clutch. A single clutch may contain as many as thirty eggs, though smaller clutches of ten to twenty eggs are more common. A variety of egg-laying patterns have been discovered. The patterns fall into two basic categories: those laid in clutches (nests) and those laid in a linear pattern along the ground, possibly by the large sauropod dinosaurs.[5]

Theropods typically laid their eggs in tight clutches with the narrow end of the elongated eggs pointed down into the ground. Parent dinosaurs created round nests with dirt walls and appear to have nested in colonies with other dinosaurs of their own kind. We do not know if the eggs were covered or how long they took to hatch. These nests may have been covered

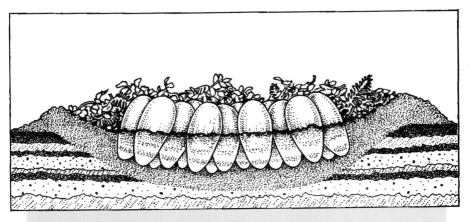

A nest of *Troodon* eggs shows that theropods laid their eggs with the narrow end pointing down into the ground.

with fresh vegetation that would gradually rot, providing incubating warmth to the eggs inside.[6]

On rare occasions, a fossil can tell us something about the way a dinosaur behaved. Two remarkable discoveries in the 1990s have provided clues that theropod parents took care of their eggs. Both dinosaur nests, one found in Montana and one in Mongolia, include fossilized adult dinosaurs found in a nesting or brooding position, protecting a clutch of eggs of its own kind.

The first of these discoveries, made by explorers from the American Museum of Natural History in 1994, included the bones of the 9-foot (2.7-meter) theropod *Oviraptor* ("egg thief") seated atop a clutch of eggs. Its arms were spread over the nest in a protective manner. Its legs were tucked beneath its body in a posture similar to that seen in nesting chickens and pigeons. Some of the eggs were crushed, but scientists estimate that there were fifteen to twenty-two eggs arranged in a circular pattern.[7]

Just what the *Oviraptor* was doing cannot be known for sure, but most scientists agree that it was providing some kind of protection for its eggs. It may have been brooding, or warming, the eggs like modern birds. It may have been protecting the nest from other dinosaurs or even the sudden sandstorm that apparently overtook them all and buried them. Whatever the case, it appears that this theropod dinosaur watched over its eggs.

A similar find in Montana by the Museum of the Rockies in 1996 revealed another startling fact. The nest in this case was one of many hundreds discovered by the museum. Because the nest included eggs and

A nesting oviraptorid protects its eggs.

the scattered bones of a juvenile plant-eating dinosaur *Orodromeus*, it was originally presumed that the eggs were those of this dinosaur. However, the discovery of an identifiable embryonic skeleton inside one of the eggs clearly showed that the eggs were those of *Troodon*, a small theropod. The presence of bones of *Orodromeus* suggested that an adult *Troodon* had possibly been catching the young plant eaters to feed its own young. This practice is similar to that of modern birds that bring food to their hatchlings in the nest.

Tiny Terrors

All dinosaur babies had something in common with today's reptiles: From the moment they hatched, they had all the basic features of adult dinosaurs, except in miniature. By contrast, this is not true of mammals and birds, most of which are born in a helpless state. Mammal and bird babies are often unable to see clearly, lack hair or feathers, are unable to walk or fly, and require parental care for an extended period.

Although baby dinosaurs may have received some care from their parents, they were mostly ready to rumble into the world from the day they were hatched. However, their small size may have prompted them to remain in the nest under the watchful eye of their parents. Being tiny in the dinosaur world meant that you were either in danger of being stepped on by a careless adult or the target for dinner for some other carnivore.

Baby dinosaurs possessed a certain cuteness due to the compact nature of their features while they were young. They had large heads, short faces, big eyes, and short tails, the same as you would see in a baby crocodile today. As they grew, their skulls lengthened, making their eyes smaller by comparison. Their bodies also grew larger in proportion to their heads, eventually giving them the typical look found in adult members of their species.

CHAPTER 7

FEEDING HABITS AND ADAPTATIONS

We know from their teeth and other skeletal parts such as the curved claws on the hands and feet that theropods ate meat. No one argues this idea. Some theropods have even been preserved with the remains of their last meal snuggled inside the rib cage where the stomach would have been. Paleontologists disagree, however, on whether all theropods were active hunters or whether some were scavengers.

Hunters or Scavengers?

The popular view of theropods, especially the largest ones such as *Tyrannosaurus*, is that they were active predators. However, some large predatory dinosaurs may have been mostly scavengers rather than hunters. Some paleontologists believe this about *Tyrannosaurus*. It may have been a relatively difficult task for a dinosaur as large as *Tyrannosaurus* to take down a galloping *Triceratops* ("three-horned face") or jogging hadrosaur. Its arms were small and could not have held on to prey trying to escape its grip. These small arms may have been useless during feeding, although they may have been used like meat hooks to lift and hold the large carcass of a dead animal. It may have also been difficult for the tyrant lizard king to deliver a single death bite to a large prey, such as a horned dinosaur. Unless it held and violently shook its victim with its jaws, it would have had trouble getting another good bite out of a squirming, 6-ton *Triceratops* without getting injured or becoming too tired to continue the pursuit.[1]

These arguments about the scavenging nature of *Tyrannosaurus* are interesting but cannot be proven. It seems as plain as day that *Tyrannosaurus* would have been better off avoiding the lethal horns of *Triceratops*. But *Tyrannosaurus* still had many defenseless dinosaurs to hunt, especially the duck-billed hadrosaurs. Nearly all carnivorous animals known today are both hunters and scavengers.[2] Experiments have shown that the jaws and teeth of *Tyrannosaurus* were strong enough to withstand the stresses that might occur while capturing prey.[3] It is more likely that all theropods hunted when they could but did not pass up a good juicy carcass when they came across one.[4]

Scavenging is easy to imagine. But killing must have required some energetic and risky behavior.

Killing Tactics

No one has ever seen a theropod catch its meal, but there are some good ideas about how they may have done this. Fossil

A pair of *Gorgosaurus* discovers a *Centrosaurus* carcass.

evidence provides some of the answers. Observations of living carnivores such as the big cats, members of the felid family, and predatory birds provide additional insight into the possible hunting habits of theropods.

Paleontologist Thomas Holtz has suggested three categories of killing strategies that may have been used by theropods: grapple and slash, grapple and bite, and pursue and bite. These are based on research he did on the predatory habits of modern carnivores.[5]

Grapple-and-slash predators. Grapple-and-slash predators usually wait in hiding and then seize the prey with the forelimbs after a very short chase. They kill their prey with a combination of slashes from the claws on the forelimb, bites, and ripping kicks from the hind limbs. In some cases they even suffocate the prey by using a bite to cover its nose and hold its mouth shut or by biting down on its throat. Of modern animals, large cats such as tigers and cheetahs are the best examples of grapple-and-slash predators. In theropods, the dromaeosaurs—popularly known as raptors—may have used this technique. They had shorter legs than other theropods, so it is likely that they did not chase their prey for long. Their long arms and hands, with three long, clawed fingers and a flexible wrist, gave them the ability to firmly grasp a prey animal. The curved and retractable claws on the second toe of each foot were ideal for delivering disemboweling kicks to the softer parts of the prey. It is possible that these creatures leaped at their prey, grabbing them with their hands and lashing out with their deadly feet. There is even one famous specimen showing a *Velociraptor* clasped in a death grip with a plant-eating *Protoceratops* ("first horned face"). The raptor is positioned in the way that paleontologists would expect to find in a grapple-and-slash attacker, with its feet kicking the underbelly of the small prey.[6]

Grapple-and-bite predators. Also ambushers, grapple-and-bite predators use the claws primarily to hold the prey while the jaws do the killing. Hawks, eagles, and other modern birds of prey use this technique. Large theropods other than *Tyrannosaurus* were probably of the grapple-and-bite variety. The claws were used to bring down the prey, but the primary killing weapon was the teeth.

Pursue-and-bite predators. Modern wolves, dogs, and hyenas use the pursue-and-bite technique. The prey is brought down with the jaws after a fairly long chase and killed using a combination of biting and suffocation. The claws, if used at

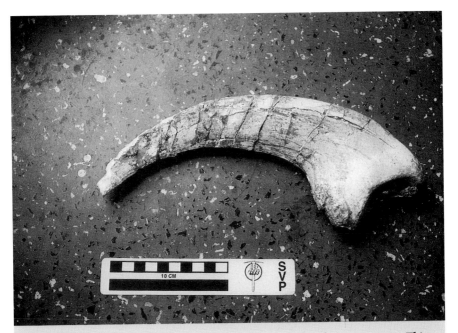

Theropod hand and foot claws were important tools for the meat eaters. This is the foot claw of *Megaraptor* from Argentina.

all, are mostly used to hold down the prey rather than slash them. Tyrannosaurs, with their long legs, huge raptorial feet, and monstrous jaws, were the theropods most likely to have used this method.

Other assumptions have been made about the way in which theropods hunted and killed. Perhaps theropods frequently attacked smaller and sickly members of a prey herd. This would lessen the risk of being injured—even a simple fall or jump by a large theropod could be disastrous, possibly breaking its legs.[7]

Attacking a large plant eater had its risks. If the herbivore was protected with horns or a sturdy tail club, the theropod might be risking its life by challenging a healthy adult. The huge weight and strength of the largest sauropods and hadrosaurs could be used to deflect or injure a pursuing predator. Although they were surefooted, theropods could not step to the side, making them vulnerable to the sideways swipe of a plant eater's heavy tail. These tails may have weighed between 1,000 and 3,000 pounds, depending on the kind of plant eater. A blow from such a tail could knock even the largest theropod over, perhaps injuring it severely, while the plant eater made its getaway.

If compelled to attack an animal much larger than itself, a theropod might choose a killing technique requiring some special tactics. First and foremost might have been the element of surprise. A theropod could lie in wait for the prey and then dash out to deliver a severe bite before getting out of harm's way. By doing this several times, a theropod might have been able to cause bleeding in a large animal that would eventually weaken it for the kill. Perhaps groups of allosaurs would use this tactic on sauropods, a tactic that has been called the hit-and-run attack.[8]

Smaller theropods that were not equipped with sickle-like foot claws probably attacked prey that was smaller than they were. They hunted mammals, reptiles, insects, or even other dinosaurs that they could easily finish off with their bites and hand claws. They may not have taken much care in chewing their meals, either. Today's largest lizard, the 10-foot (3-meter)

Komodo dragon, will swallow a whole chicken, feathers and all, in one or two swift gulps. Theropods of about the same size, such as *Coelophysis*, may have swallowed their smaller prey whole. Stomach contents of such dinosaurs, although only rarely preserved in the fossil record, have shown that small prey had been swallowed intact, without being dismembered or chewed.

Theropods as Pack Hunters

The scenario of a group of allosaurs attacking a sauropod sounds like group or pack hunting. Although theropod remains are usually found by themselves, there are several fossil sites that include more than one individual of the same kind of predatory dinosaur, implying pack or cooperative hunting.

The bones of several individuals of *Deinonychus*, a 9-foot dromaeosaur, were discovered in Montana in 1964. Because several individuals of this theropod were found near the bones of the plant eater *Tenontosaurus* ("tendon lizard"), it seems that *Deinonychus* hunted in packs. It is hard to imagine that a single *Deinonychus* could have brought down a 23-foot (7-meter) *Tenontosaurus* by itself. The teeth of *Deinonychus* were small and its jaw structure was slender and light, making the mouth better designed for cutting and slicing meat than for killing. Like other dromaeosaurs, however, *Deinonychus* was built with strong arms and legs, a grasping hand with long claws, and a menacing sickle-like claw on each foot. This dinosaur probably ganged up on larger prey, leaping and lashing out with its foot claws, mortally wounding its victim until it succumbed by bleeding to death.

There are several fossil sites where multiple theropods have died together, suggesting that they traveled in a group that may have hunted. There is a famous *Coelophysis* quarry at Ghost Ranch, New Mexico, that includes the remains of over a thousand adult and juvenile individuals of this small meat eater. They died at the same time, presumably victims of a mass drowning, yet they were apparently traveling together.[9] What they were doing together is still a mystery. The group is clearly larger than a hunting pack. They may have been migrating or seeking refuge from some natural disaster. Whatever the reason, small packs of these creatures could easily have broken off to seek prey together.

Evidence that some of the largest theropods may have traveled in groups has also been found. A site in western Canada contains nine individuals of the tyrannosaur *Albertosaurus* ("Alberta lizard") that suddenly perished. The group consisted of juveniles and adults and is considered by paleontologist Phil Currie to have been a hunting pack. In imagining their behavior, Currie suggests that the swifter juveniles might have gone ahead of the pack to chase down and trouble a prey group, such as hadrosaurs. They would eventually single out individuals and distract them until the adults could arrive to make the kill.[10]

In addition to the albertosaur site, there is a fossil location in Patagonia, Argentina, that also includes several individuals of the largest theropod ever found. Located in the province of

An *Albertosaurus* pack hunt proves to be successful, as they close in on a *Hypacrosaurus*.

Neuquén, the site of this yet-unnamed new theropod includes up to six individuals ranging from juveniles to adults. The largest individual may be the largest theropod ever discovered and is similar to *Giganotosaurus*, also found in the same region.[11]

Whether pack hunting existed in dinosaurs is controversial. Pack hunting in mammals is an organized activity requiring high intelligence. Assuming that dinosaur brains were mostly on a scale with modern reptiles and not mammals, it is not likely that they displayed all of the complex tactics and cooperative hunting behaviors seen in today's mammals. However, there is no question that theropods seemed to have traveled in groups. It is likely that this led to some level of cooperative hunting or communal attacking of prey.

Toxic Teeth

Another intriguing idea about theropod killing methods suggests that the mouths of large predatory dinosaurs were filled with bacteria from past meals, bacteria to which the individual theropod would have become immune. The bacteria would have been trapped in pockets between the dinosaurs' teeth. When they bit their prey and the prey escaped, the victim would have become infected by the bacteria. This might not have killed the prey, but it could have weakened it enough for the theropod to catch up with it later. The theropod could have followed the wounded prey for as long as it took to drop, tracking it by the smell of the infected wound.[12] It has been suggested that the jagged edges of *Tyrannosaurus* teeth provided sufficient gaps between the individual denticles to hold small particles of meat, allowing such bacteria to thrive. A similar technique has been observed in the killing methods of today's Komodo dragon.[13]

What Did They Eat?

There are several good clues in the fossil record for the kinds of things that theropods ate. Judging from tooth marks sometimes found on their bones, sauropods, hadrosaurs, and horned dinosaurs seem to have been popular meals with the larger predators such as *Allosaurus*, *Albertosaurus*, and *Tyrannosaurus*. This is proven by evidence found in fossilized

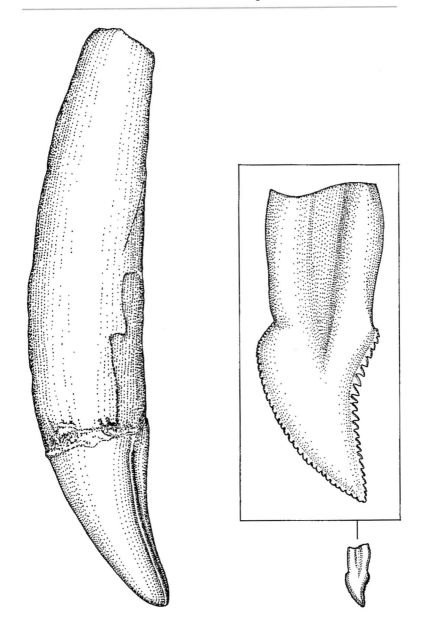

Serrated teeth were characteristic of all theropods (*Tyrannosaurus*, left, *Troodon*, right). Such teeth were designed for shredding and slicing meat.

dung—called *coprolite*—of large theropods that were probably tyrannosaurs. One coprolite contains small bone fragments from a plant-eating dinosaur. The plant eater was possibly the horned dinosaur *Torvosaurus* ("savage lizard"), the 11-foot (3.3-meter) *Thescelosaurus* ("wonderful lizard"), or another yet unidentified herbivore from the same region of Saskatchewan, Canada, where the coprolite was discovered.[14] The fact that the bone fragments were small and pulverized tells scientists something about the way in which *T. rex* ate. Because of its large, pointed teeth, it is not likely that the theropod could have ground down the bone by chewing it. Predator tooth marks found on specimens of *Triceratops* provide evidence of another eating method. It appears that *T. rex* scraped its teeth along the fleshy parts of the prey's body, shredding off strips of meat as it did so. This left a series of parallel grooves in the bone of the animal as the teeth dug down to the skeleton. The fragments of crushed bone found in the fossilized *T. rex* dropping were probably scraped up by the teeth as the dinosaur pulled its jaws across the prey like a cob of corn.[15]

A second tyrannosaur coprolite, discovered in 1998, includes fossilized fragments of undigested muscle fiber. This evidence gives paleontologists an unusual glimpse of theropod eating habits. Perhaps the dinosaur had gorged itself and excreted part of its meal undigested. This may have been how theropods often behaved when eating.[16]

Some theropod skeletons have been found with the remains of their last meal still inside the rib cage. This remarkable evidence provides firsthand information about dinosaur

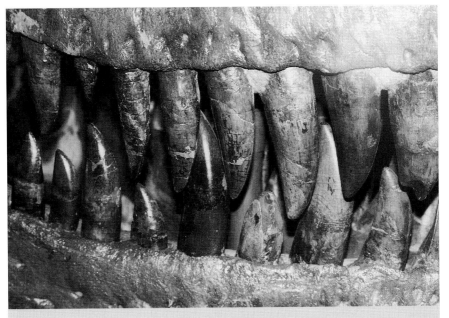

Tyrannosaurus rex teeth

meals. One skeleton of the chicken-sized *Compsognathus* revealed the tiny bones of a small lizard in its rib cage.[17]

The shape of the jaw of *Baryonyx* ("strong claw") and the number of teeth (twice as many in the lower jaw than other kinds of theropods) suggests that it may have been piscivorous, meaning that it ate fish. Its long hand claws also seem well suited to snagging fish in a stream. The clincher came with the discovery of fossilized fish remains in a *Baryonyx* body cavity.[18]

In 1999, a specimen of *Daspletosaurus* ("frightful lizard") was discovered that included the partially digested bones of a juvenile hadrosaur in its stomach area. This confirms that duck-billed dinosaurs were the prey of tyrannosaurs.[19] The fact that the hadrosaur was young also suggests that it had been alive when the tyrannosaur ate it, evidence that large theropods were active hunters at least part of the time.

Those theropods without teeth—the ostrichlike ornithomimosaurs and oviraptors—probably ate large insects and small vertebrates such as reptiles and amphibians. They may have even indulged in a small furry mammal on occasion.

There is even proof of cannibalism in dinosaurs. Two of the hundreds of *Coelophysis* specimens discovered in New Mexico each contain the remains of a young *Coelophysis* in its stomach; evidence that theropods were not always discriminating about what they ate. Did theropods normally eat their young? Certainly not—survival of the species would have been quite difficult if this happened most of the time. However, it seems that *Coelophysis*, like the modern crocodile, occasionally dined on younger members of its own kind.[20]

CHAPTER 8

EXTINCTION OF THE DINOSAURS

The last of the dinosaurs became extinct 65 million years ago. However, they did not disappear because they were evolutionary failures. Dinosaurs were one of the most successful forms of life ever to inhabit our planet. They ruled the earth for 160 million years. Humans, by comparison, and even our most distant relatives, have been around for only about 4 million years.

Extinction is the irreversible elimination of an entire species of plant or animal. Once it occurs, there is no turning back. It is also a natural process. More than 99 percent of all the species of organisms that have ever lived are now extinct.[1]

Although dinosaurs existed for so many millions of years, most species existed for only a few million years at a time, until they became extinct or were replaced by "improved" models. So, to say that all the dinosaurs became extinct at the end of the Cretaceous Period is incorrect—most kinds of dinosaurs had already come and gone by then. There is no denying, however, that a mass extinction occurred at the end of the Cretaceous that wiped out about 65 to 70 percent of all animal life.[2] Even those groups of animals that survived, including frogs, lizards, turtles, salamanders, birds, insects, fish, crocodiles, alligators, and mammals, lost great numbers of their species.

Chief among the causes of animal extinction are environmental changes that affect their food supply or body chemistry (such as extreme temperatures), disease, and natural disasters (such as volcanic eruptions, earthquakes, and the changing surface of the earth). Extensive hunting by natural enemies may also contribute to extinction. Humankind, for example, has hunted many animals such as the buffalo to extinction or near extinction.

Why did the last of the dinosaurs become extinct? This is a great mystery of science.

The death of the dinosaurs is difficult to explain because dinosaurs were part of a strangely selective extinction event. Any suitable explanation must account for the disappearance of dinosaurs as well as flying reptiles, reptiles that swam in the oceans, and ammonites and other sea creatures, including some types of clams, mollusks, and plankton. It must also explain why so many other types of animals continued to thrive after that event.

Paleontologists disagree on the causes of dinosaur extinction and the length of time it took for this mass dying to occur. There are many theories about what happened. They come in two basic varieties: gradual causes and sudden causes.

Theories of Dinosaur Extinction

THEORY	TYPE OF THEORY	PROBLEMS WITH THE THEORY
The Big Rumble Smoke and dust spewed by mass volcanic eruptions shrouded the earth in darkness, killing plants, poisoning the air and water, and causing the climate to cool.	Gradual	Does not explain why other land- and ocean-dwelling animals survived.
Shifting Continents Planetary cooling caused by shifting continents and changes to the earth's oceans. Water between the land masses would have cooled the air and caused wind.	Gradual	This happened very slowly. Why couldn't dinosaurs and marine reptiles have adapted to the climate change or moved to warmer climates?
Pesky Mammals New mammals stole and ate dinosaur eggs.	Gradual	Does not explain why some sea life became extinct or why other egg-laying land animals such as snakes and lizards survived. Also, small mammals coexisted with dinosaurs for many millions of year without this happening.
Flower Poisoning Flowers first appeared during the Cretaceous Period. Were dinosaurs unable to adapt to the chemical makeup of this new source of food?	Gradual	Plant-eating dinosaurs actually increased in diversity and numbers during the rise of the flowering plants.
Bombardment from Space Impact by an asteroid or comet shrouded the earth in darkness from debris thrown into the atmosphere and may have poisoned the air. Plants died and the climate cooled.	Sudden	Does not explain the survival of some land reptiles, mammals, birds, amphibians, and plants, or why certain ocean life perished but not others.
Supernova Explosion of a nearby star bathed the earth in deadly cosmic rays.	Sudden	Why did some life-forms die and not others?

Gradual causes would have required millions of years of change. Some possible gradual causes include global climate changes (warming or cooling), volcanic action, shifting continents, overpopulation, poisoning by flowering plants, and the appearance of egg-stealing mammals.

Sudden or catastrophic causes would have taken no longer than a few years to wipe out the dinosaurs. Popular theories for a rapid extinction include disease and the collision of an asteroid or comet with the earth.

So far, no single extinction theory can fully explain the great dying at the end of the age of dinosaurs. Evidence has been mounting in favor of the asteroid theory. But a collision with an asteroid may have been only the final blow in a gradual extinction that had been mounting for many years. The asteroid theory also fails to explain why the extinction was so selective. Why did marine reptiles die but most fish survive? Why did dinosaurs of all sizes disappear but birds continue to thrive? There are still many questions to answer before we totally understand this great mystery.

CHAPTER 9

MAJOR THEROPOD DISCOVERIES

Unlike many older sciences, such as mathematics and astronomy, paleontology is quite young. This chapter summarizes the major discoveries of predatory dinosaurs and the people who made them during the last two centuries.

✦ ✦ ✦

1822–1824 (England)—Physician and amateur geologist **James Parkinson** discovered the fragmentary remains of a large theropod dinosaur in Stonesfield. The specimen included the right half of the lower jaw and teeth. He recognized it as an extinct "saurian" and was the first to name a theropod dinosaur. He called it *Megalosaurus* ("great lizard"). It became the first dinosaur to be described scientifically when professor **William Buckland** wrote about it in 1824. Still poorly known, the genus *Megalosaurus* was for many years a convenient category for dumping other poorly known large theropods.

✦ ✦ ✦

1842 (England)—British anatomist **Richard Owen**, having recognized the differences between *Iguanodon*, *Megalosaurus*, and other large, extinct saurians described by that time, created the term *Dinosauria* ("terrible lizards") as a means for scientifically classifying the unique animals. This is the origin of the word *dinosaur*.

✦ ✦ ✦

1856 (United States)—Joseph Leidy, an anatomist and paleontologist in Philadelphia, described the first four dinosaurs positively identified in America. The specimens consisted only of teeth that were recovered by an expedition led by **Ferdinand Vandiveer Hayden** into the Montana territory. But Leidy's keen diagnostic eye recognized the special nature of these specimens. Four dinosaurs were named: *Troodon* ("wounding tooth"), *Trachodon* ("rough tooth"), *Palaeoscincus* ("ancient skink"), and *Deinodon* ("terror tooth"). *Troodon* and *Deinodon* were theropods.

1861 (Germany)—A remarkably complete fossil of the chicken-sized theropod *Compsognathus* ("elegant jaw") was described by **Andreas Wagner**. It was discovered in the fine-grained limestone deposits of Solnhofen in Germany. *Compsognathus* was complete except for the end of the tail, and for the first time the general anatomy shared by most theropods was revealed. It was long-legged and swift, with tiny curved and pointed teeth. It is known from only two specimens.

In the same year, **Hermann von Meyer** published a description of the earliest known bird ancestor, *Archaeopteryx* ("ancient wing"). It was also discovered in the exquisite limestone deposits of Solnhofen, Germany. The fossil was remarkable for showing a skeleton resembling that of *Compsognathus* with wings and feathers. Unlike modern birds, *Archaeopteryx* had teeth, a reptilian feature. It was immediately hailed by some as the "missing link" between dinosaurs and birds.

1866 (United States)—Philadelphia paleontologist **Edward Drinker Cope** described the most complete specimen of an American theropod discovered to date. He named it *Laelaps* ("storm wind," after the mythical hunting dog of the same name) because he pictured it as a lively, active predator, lashing out with its deadly hand and foot claws. The dinosaur was lightly built and had the hollow bones characteristic of theropods. It had huge claws comparable to those of the giant raptor *Utahraptor*. It was probably between 15 and 20 feet (4.6 and 6 meters) long. Unfortunately for Cope, the scientific name *Laelaps* had already been used for a spider.[1] Noticing this, his archrival dinosaur hunter **Othniel Charles Marsh** of Yale University renamed the dinosaur *Dryptosaurus* ("tearing lizard"), the official name that sticks to this day.

1868 (England)—Thomas H. Huxley was a biologist and supporter of **Charles Darwin**'s theory of evolution, published only nine years prior. Huxley wrote a paper describing the similarities between *Compsognathus* and other dinosaurs to *Archaeopteryx*, suggesting that birds were descended from dinosaurs.[2] This once-accepted theory went out of favor during the early part of the twentieth century, but it has now become widely accepted again.

✦ ✦ ✦

1877 (United States)—Othniel Charles Marsh named *Allosaurus* ("other lizard"), the largest predatory dinosaur known at that time. Curiously, Marsh's arch rival **Cope** had found a more complete specimen of the same dinosaur prior to Marsh but had not had time to examine it before Marsh had found, and named, his own specimen.

✦ ✦ ✦

1890 (United States)—Marsh named *Ornithomimus* ("bird mimic"), a theropod with a body design like the modern ostrich. It was found in Colorado and was the first of the ostrich dinosaurs discovered. A skull for this dinosaur, which was beaklike and toothless, was not discovered until 1915, when one was found by fossil hunter **George Sternberg** in Canada.

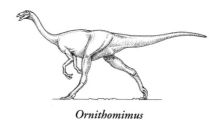

Ornithomimus

1905 (United States)—Henry Fairfield Osborn described *Tyrannosaurus* ("tyrant lizard"), the largest known predatory dinosaur at that time. The specimen was discovered by famed fossil collector **Barnum Brown** in Montana and was about 50 percent complete. He was working for Osborn and the American Museum of Natural History in New York City. A second, larger, and more complete specimen was also found by Brown within a few years. For a time, the American Museum was home to two excellent specimens of the "tyrant lizard king." Legend has it that as World War II ensued, and fear grew that New York City might be bombed, the museum decided to part with one of its cherished *rexes* in order to safeguard at least one of them. They sold the original specimen, which was less complete, to the Carnegie Museum in Pittsburgh, where it is still on exhibit.[3]

1905 (Canada)—Henry Fairfield Osborn of the American Museum of Natural History named *Albertosaurus* ("Alberta lizard"), a 29-foot- (8.8-meter-) long tyrannosaur that was similar to *Tyrannosaurus*, but more lightly built. It was discovered in western Canada in the province of Alberta.

1914 (Canada)—Lawrence Lambe described the large meat-eater *Gorgosaurus* ("fierce lizard") found in Alberta. It was a two-fingered meat eater related to *Tyrannosaurus* but somewhat smaller. Until recently, it was thought to be the same dinosaur as *Albertosaurus* from the same area. However, recent work by paleontologist **Phil Currie** on new specimens of *Albertosaurus* clearly shows that it is different than *Gorgosaurus*.[4]

✦ ✦ ✦

1915 (Africa)—The large sail-backed theropod *Spinosaurus* ("spiny lizard") was discovered in Egypt and named by German **Ernst Stromer**. Measuring up to 50 feet (15 meters) long, this enormous theropod had a sail running down its back that may have been as tall as 6.5 feet (2 meters). Unfortunately, this incredible specimen, which had been housed in Germany, was destroyed by bombing during World War II.

✦ ✦ ✦

1917 (Canada)—Legendary head of the fossil collecting Sternberg clan, **Charles Sternberg** discovered what turned out to be the most complete skeleton of a North American

Gorgosaurus juvenile

predatory dinosaur known at that time, called *Albertosaurus* ("Alberta lizard"). *Albertosaurus* is a tyrannosaur, smaller than *Tyrannosaurus*.

✦ ✦ ✦

1922 (Canada)—The first described dromaeosaur, *Dromaeosaurus* ("swift lizard"), was christened by **William D. Matthew** and **Barnum Brown**.

✦ ✦ ✦

1922–1924 (Mongolia)—A fossil hunting expedition headed by **Roy Chapman Andrews** of the American Museum of Natural History discovered the first positive evidence of dinosaur nests and eggs. These were attributed to the plant-eating *Protoceratops* ("first horned face"). In 1923, the explorers discovered the remains of the small theropod dinosaur *Oviraptor* in close proximity to egg nests. At the time is was believed that *Oviraptor*, whose name means "egg thief," was probably gobbling down the eggs of the *Protoceratops*. However, in 1994, **Mark Norell** and his colleagues from the American Museum revealed that some of the eggs contained the remains of *Oviraptor* embryos, making these the first eggs positively associated with a specific theropod.[5]

Another important theropod discovered by the team in 1923 was the small dromaeosaur *Velociraptor* ("swift thief"). One of its sickle claws was found in association with its well-preserved skull, but no one could tell that the claw came from one of its feet. The true nature of this killing machine was unknown until later specimens were found in the 1960s.

Finally, the expedition also uncovered an excellent specimen of *Saurornitholestes* ("lizard bird-robber"), which was related to the North American predatory dinosaur *Troodon*.

1946–1949 (Mongolia)—Following the example of the Americans over twenty years earlier, a team of Russian paleontologists conducted several expeditions to Mongolia in search of dinosaurs. Led by **Ivan Antonovich Efremov**, the expeditions uncovered many intriguing new dinosaurs, including ten specimens of the tyrannosaur *Tarbosaurus* ("terrible lizard") and the strange long-armed theropod *Therizinosaurus* ("scythe lizard"), which was outfitted with huge 30-inch (76-centimeter) claws on its hands.

1947 (United States)—Edwin H. Colbert and a team from the American Museum of Natural History discovered a bone bed in New Mexico containing hundreds of specimens of *Coelophysis* ("hollow form"). This small theropod from the Late Triassic was one of the earliest dinosaurs. It was originally named by **Cope** in 1889 based on fragmentary material. Colbert's studies of this small, agile theropod make this one of the best understood of all dinosaurs.

1963 (Argentina)—Paleontologist **Osvaldo A. Reig** of the National University at Tucumán described *Herrerasaurus* ("Herrera's lizard"), a possible early ancestor of the first dinosaurs. It was found in northwestern Argentina.

1963-1971 (Mongolia)—The Polish-Mongolian Expeditions, like the Russian and American ones before them, set out to explore the vast fossil-rich plains of the Gobi Desert and other parts of Mongolia. Led by female paleontologist **Zofia Kielan-Jaworowska** of the Paleozoological Institute of the Polish Academy of Sciences, various teams made five such expeditions. As for theropods, additional remains of *Tarbosaurus* were discovered, as well as the gigantic 8-foot (2.4-meter) arms of *Deinocheirus* ("terrible hand"), a mysterious creature about which we know nothing else. Others included the ostrich dinosaur *Gallimimus* ("rooster mimic"), and a dinosaur with many similarities to birds named *Avimimus* ("bird mimic"). Perhaps the most spectacular find was that of a *Velociraptor* engaged in a death grip with a *Protoceratops*. The horned dinosaur was biting the predator's limb while the raptor attempted to slash at the belly of its prey with its sickle-clawed feet. This provided a rare glimpse not only of two rival dinosaur skeletons but of their behavior as well.[6]

1969 (United States)—**John Ostrom** of Yale University described a new theropod from Montana which he named *Deinonychus* ("terrible claw"). This 9-foot- (2.7-meter-) long predator was significant because its anatomy suggested that it was swift, agile, and possibly warm-blooded. This view of dinosaurs was not popular with most scientists at the time. Ostrom extended his research of *Deinonychus* to suggest that it and other dromaeosaurs like it were probably the direct ancestors of birds. Ostrom's work was largely responsible for the rebirth of interest in dinosaurs that has occurred since then.

1969 (Africa)—The Late Triassic theropod *Syntarsus* ("fused ankle") was discovered by **M. A. Raath** in Zimbabwe. This early 10-foot- (3-meter-) long, lightweight predator has also been found in Arizona, demonstrating that dinosaurs had migrated across the supercontinent Pangaea (when the continents as we know them today were still joined).

1970 (Brazil)—Another possible early ancestor of the dinosaurs, *Staurikosaurus* ("cross lizard"), was named by **Edwin H. Colbert**. It was found in southern Brazil.

1985 (Argentina)—**José Bonaparte** described the large abelisaurid theropod *Carnotaurus* ("bull lizard"), which sported two prominent horns on top of its head and had unusually short, three-fingered forelimbs.

1986 (England)—**Alan Charig** and **Angela Milner** named *Baryonyx* ("strong claw"), a fish-eating spinosaurid found in Surrey. It had the remains of an ancient fish in its rib cage, indicating that it was piscivorous. It had large claws on its hands, probably to help snag fish.

1986–1990 (China and Canada)—The China-Canadian Dinosaur Project involved a series of highly successful expeditions involving Chinese and Canadian paleontologists. Leaders of the project included **Phil Currie** (Canada) and **Dong Zhiming** (China). Several remarkable theropods were discovered. *Sinraptor* ("China robber") stalked the Late Jurassic plains of Mongolia and was about 24 feet (7.3 meters) long. It is important because it fills a gap in the evolution of large theropods in China. *Monolophosaurus* ("single-crested lizard") was a 17-foot- (5.2-meter-) long predator with a 5-inch- (13-centimeter-) tall crest decorating the top of its nose and head. It was found in rocks of Middle Jurassic age in China.[7]

1993 (United States)—**James Kirkland** named *Utahraptor* ("Utah thief"), the largest known member of the dromaeosaur family. These agile, predatory dinosaurs are equipped with killing claws on their feet. *Utahraptor* measures about 20 feet (6 meters) long.

1990–1993 (Argentina)—**Paul Sereno** and **Catherine Forster** of the University of Chicago, among others, collaborated with Argentinean scientists **José Bonaparte**, **Fernando Novas**, and **Andrea Arcucci** to explore the Late Triassic deposits of Argentina for early dinosaurs. Among their finds were additional remains of *Herrerasaurus* and a new early theropod ancestor *Eoraptor* ("dawn thief").

1993 (Antarctica)—**William Hammer** of Augustana College in Illinois named the first dinosaur to be described

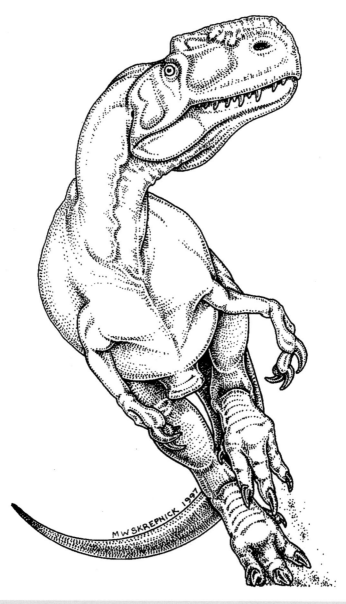

Monolophosaurus, a Chinese theropod with an enlarged nasal crest, was 17 feet (5.2 meters) long.

from Antarctica, which confirmed that dinosaurs were to be found on all seven continents. The Early Jurassic medium-sized theropod was named *Cryolophosaurus* ("cool crested lizard"). It was notable for the unusual curved crest on its head.

✦ ✦ ✦

1994 (Mongolia)—Mark Norell and other explorers from the American Museum of Natural History discovered the remains of an *Oviraptor* lying in a brooding position on a nest of eggs. This discovery provided evidence for parental care in theropod dinosaurs.[8]

✦ ✦ ✦

1994–1995 (Africa)—Three new theropods were discovered in Africa by a team from the University of Chicago headed by **Paul Sereno**. *Afrovenator* ("Africa hunter"), a large meat eater, was discovered in Niger in 1994. This 28-foot (8.5-meter) predator was related to *Torvosaurus* ("savage lizard") from North America and dates from the Early Cretaceous Period. The following year, while exploring in Morocco, the team discovered a huge skull from the previously known *Carcharodontosaurus* ("sharp-toothed lizard"), an abelisaurid theropod that rivals *T. rex* in size. They also found a large but lightly built terror called *Deltadromeus* ("delta runner"), which measured about 28 feet, 9 inches (8.8 meters) long. These finds, and more to come, are greatly expanding our knowledge of African dinosaurs.

1995 (Argentina)—*Giganotosaurus* ("gigantic southern lizard"), a huge theropod related to *Carcharodontosaurus* in Africa, was named by **Rodolfo Coria** and **Leonardo Salgado** of the Carmen Funes Museum in Plaza Huincul. It was as big or bigger than *Tyrannosaurus*, but it had a lighter, longer skull and teeth that were more slender and bladelike.

1996 (China)—A dinosaur embryo associated with large elongated eggs once thought to belong to a tyrannosaur was discovered. The embryonic skeleton proved to be a therizinosaur, an unusual and rare theropod with long arms and huge claws on its hands. This find was studied by American **Ken Carpenter** of the Denver Museum and **Phil Currie** of the Royal Tyrrell Museum of Palaeontology in Canada. It dates from the Late Cretaceous of Henan province.[9]

1996 (China)—**Chen Peiji** of the Nanjing Paleontology Institute and **Phil Currie** of the Royal Tyrrell Museum of Palaeontology in Canada revealed the discovery of a "downy" dinosaur from the Liaoning province of China. Preserved in a fine-grained sandstone slab, the small creature now known as *Sinosauropteryx* ("Chinese ancient wing") appeared to have fibrous or downy structures running along its spine.

1997 (Argentina)—**Fernando Novas**, of the Argentina Museum of Natural History in Buenos Aires, described a new theropod from the Late Cretaceous, *Unenlagia* ("half bird").

The most remarkable feature of this 7.5-foot- (2.3-meter-) long predator is not its size or teeth or arsenal of weapons. It had long, unusual arms that could be held in a winglike way, folded so that the upper arm bone could lie close to the body like a bird's. It combines many features of both birds and dinosaurs and may help to show how terrestrial dinosaur arms evolved to become bird wings.

1998 (China)—The controversial small theropod named *Sinosauropteryx* was described by **Chen Peiji, Dong Zhiming, and Zhen Shuonan**. It was the first small dinosaur from the Liaoning province of China that hinted at the presence of feathers.[10] Its back and neck were covered with small fibers that may have been some kind of down or "dino fuzz." Originally thought to predate the appearance of *Archaeopteryx*, it was later determined that this dinosaur and others found at the same location were probably about 20 million years younger than the first bird. This falsified the original claim that *Sinosauropteryx* was probably an ancestor of early birds.

1998 (China)—**Ji Qiang, Phil Currie, Mark Norell, and Ji Shunan** describe the first definitive specimens of theropod dinosaurs with feathers. The two startling specimens of small theropods are called *Protarchaeopteryx* ("before *Archaeopteryx*") and *Caudipteryx* ("tail feather").[11]

Suchomimus, an African meat eater with a crocodile-like snout

1998 (Africa)—**Paul Sereno** discovered a new member of the spinosaurid family in Niger. Called *Suchomimus* ("crocodile mimic"), this long-snouted theropod had a mouth similar to that of a crocodile on a two-legged, 37-foot (11-meter) body. It was related to *Baryonyx* from England and is presumed to have eaten fish.

CURRENTLY KNOWN THEROPODS

The list below includes the genus names of currently known and scientifically accepted theropods. Each genus name is followed by the name(s) of the paleontologist(s) who described the animal in print and the year in which it was named.

Abelisaurus—Bonaparte and Novas, 1985

Acrocanthosaurus—Stovall and Langston, 1950

Adasaurus—Barsbold, 1983

Afrovenator—Sereno, Wilson, Larsson, Dutheil, and Sues, 1994

Albertosaurus—Osborn, 1905

Alectrosaurus—Gilmore, 1933

Alioramus—Kurzanov, 1976

Aliwalia—Galton, 1985

Allosaurus—Marsh, 1877

Altispinax—Huene, 1923

Alvarezsaurus—Bonaparte, 1991

Alwalkeria—Chatterjee and Creisler, 1994

Alxasaurus—Russell and Dong, 1993

Anserimimus—Barsbold, 1988

Archaeornithomimus—Russell, 1972

Avimimus—Kurzanov, 1981

Baryonyx—Charig and Milner, 1986

Becklespinax—Olshevsky, 1991

Beipiaosaurus—Xu Xing, Tang Zhilu, and Wang, 1999

Borogovia—Osmolska, 1987

Caenagnathasia—Currie, Godfrey, and Nessov, 1993

Caenagnathus—R. M. Sternberg, 1940

Carcharodontosaurus—Stromer, 1931

Carnotaurus—Bonaparte and Coria, 1985

Caudipteryx—Ji Qiang, Currie, Norell, Ji, 1998

Ceratosaurus—Marsh, 1884

Chilantaisaurus—Hu, 1964

Chindesaurus—Long and Murray, 1995

Chingkankousaurus—Young, 1958

Chirostenotes—Gilmore, 1924

Coelophysis—Cope, 1889

Coelurus—Marsh, 1879

Compsognathus—Wagner, 1861

Conchoraptor—Barsbold, 1986

Cryolophosaurus—Hammer and Hickerson, 1994

Daspletosaurus—Russell, 1970

Deinocheirus—Osmólska and Roniewicz, 1970

Deinonychus—Ostrom, 1969

Deltadromeus—Sereno, 1995

Dilophosaurus—Welles, 1970

Dromaeosaurus—Matthew and Brown, 1922

Dromiceiomimus—Russell, 1972

Dryptosaurus—Marsh, 1877

Elmisaurus—Osmolska, 1981

Eoraptor—Sereno, Forster, Rogers, and Monetta, 1993

Erectopus—Huene, 1921

Frenguellisaurus—Novas, 1986

Gallimimus—Osmolska, Roniewicz, and Barsbold, 1972

Garudimimus—Barsbold, 1981

Genusaurus—Accarie, Beaudoin, Dejax, Fries, Michard, and
          Taquet, 1995

Genyodectes—Woodward, 1901

Giganotosaurus—Coria and Salgado, 1995
Harpymimus—Barsbold and Perle, 1984
Herrerasaurus—Reig, 1963
Hulsanpes—Osmolska, 1982
Indosaurus—Huene and Matley, 1933
Indosuchus—Huene and Matley, 1933
Ingenia—Barsbold, 1981
Ischisaurus—Reig, 1963
Itemirus—Kurzanov, 1976
Liliensternus—Welles, 1984
Majungasaurus—Lavocat, 1954
Majungatholus—Sues and Taquet, 1979
Maleevosaurus—Carpenter, 1992
Marshosaurus—Madsen, 1976
Megalosaurus—Buckland, 1824
Metriacanthosaurus—Walker, 1964
Monolophosaurus—Zhao and Currie, 1993
Mononykus—Perle, Norell, and Chiappe, 1993
Nanotyrannus—Bakker, Currie, and Williams, 1988
Ornitholestes—Osborn, 1903
Ornithomimus—Marsh, 1890
Oviraptor—Osborn, 1924
Pelecanimimus—Perez-Moreno, Sanz, Buscalioni, Moratalla,
            Ortega, and Rasskin-Gutman, 1994
Piatnitzkysaurus—Bonaparte, 1979
Poekilopleuron—Eudes-Deslongchamps, 1838
Proceratosaurus—Huene, 1926
Protarchaeopteryx—Ji, Currie, Norell, Ji, 1998
Rapator—Huene, 1932
Sarcosaurus—Andrews, 1921
Saurophaganax—Chure, 1995
Saurornithoides—Osborn, 1924

Saurornitholestes—Sues, 1978

Segisaurus—Camp, 1936

Shanshanosaurus—Dong, 1977

Shuvosaurus—Chatterjee, 1993

Siamotyrannus—Buffetaut et al, 1996

Sinornithoides—Russell and Dong, 1993

Sinosauropteryx—Chen, Dong, and Zhen, 1998

Sinraptor—Currie and Zhao, 1993

Spinosaurus—Stromer, 1915

Spondylosoma—Huene, 1942

Staurikosaurus—Colbert, 1970

Struthiomimus—Osborn, 1917

Suchomimus—Sereno, et al 1998

Syntarsus—Raath, 1969

Szechuanosaurus—Young, 1942

Tarascosaurus—Le Loeuff and Buffetaut, 1991

Tarbosaurus—Maleev, 1955

Therizinosaurus—Maleev, 1954

Tochisaurus—Kurzanov and Osmólska, 1991

Torvosaurus—Galton and Jensen, 1979

Troodon—Leidy, 1856

Tyrannosaurus—Osborn, 1905

Unenlagia—Novas, 1997

Unquillosaurus—Powell, 1979

Utahraptor—Kirkland, Burge, and Gaston, 1993

Valdoraptor—Olshevsky, 1991

Velociraptor—Osborn, 1924

Velocisaurus—Bonaparte, 1991

Xenotarsosaurus—Martinez, Gimenez, Rodriquez, and Bochatey, 1987

Xuanhanosaurus—Dong, 1984

Yangchuanosaurus—Dong, Zhou, Chang, and Li, 1978

CHAPTER NOTES

Chapter 1. Dinosaurs Defined

1. Peter Dodson and Susan D. Dawson, "Making the Fossil Record of Dinosaurs," *Modern Geology*, vol. 16, 1991, p. 13.

2. Philip J. Currie and Kevin Padian, eds., *The Encyclopedia of Dinosaurs* (San Diego, Calif.: Academic Press, 1997), p. 731.

Chapter 2. Origins and Evolution

1. David B. Weishampel, Peter Dodson, and Halszka Osmólska, eds., *The Dinosauria* (Berkeley, Calif.: University of California Press, 1990), p. 11.

2. Paul Sereno, "The Evolution of Dinosaurs," *Science*, June 25, 1999, vol. 284, p. 2137.

3. Ibid.

4. David E. Fastovsky and David B. Weishampel, *The Evolution and Extinction of the Dinosaurs* (Cambridge, England: Cambridge University Press, 1996), pp. 272–273.

5. Based on Sereno, pp. 2137–2147.

Chapter 4. Anatomy

1. Stephen Jay Gould, ed., *The Book of Life* (New York: W. W. Norton & Company, 1993), pp. 67–68.

2. David B. Weishampel, Peter Dodson, and Halszka Osmólska, eds., *The Dinosauria* (Berkeley, Calif.: University of California Press, 1990), p. 213.

3. Ibid., pp. 172, 259–261.

Chapter 5. Physiology

1. Philip J. Currie and Kevin Padian, eds., *The Encyclopedia of Dinosaurs* (San Diego, Calif.: Academic Press, 1997), p. 371.

2. R. D. K. Thomas and E. C. Olson, eds., *A Cold Look at the Warm-Blooded Dinosaurs* (Washington, D.C.: American Association for the Advancement of Science, *Selected Symposium no. 28*, 1980), pp. 287–310.

3. David E. Fastovsky and David B. Weishampel, *The Evolution and Extinction of the Dinosaurs* (Cambridge, England: Cambridge University Press, 1996), p. 339.

4. David B. Weishampel, Peter Dodson, and Halszka Osmólska, eds., *The Dinosauria* (Berkeley, Calif.: University of California Press, 1990), p. 213.

5. Gregory S. Paul, *Predatory Dinosaurs of the World* (New York: Simon and Schuster, 1988), p. 100.

6. Philip J. Currie, "Cranial Anatomy of *Stenonychosaurus inequalis* (Saurischia, Theropoda) and its Bearing on the Origin of Birds," *Canadian Journal of Earth Sciences*, vol. 22, 1985, pp. 1643–1658.

7. Donavan Webster, "A Dinosaur Named Sue," *National Geographic*, June 1999, pp. 48–49.

8. Anusuya Chinsamy, "Physiological Implications of the Bone Histology of *Syntarsus rhodesiensis* (Saurischia: Theropoda)," *Palaeontologia Africana*, vol. 27, 1990, pp.77–82.

9. David J. Varricchio and John R. Horner, "Hadrosaurid and Lambeosaurid Bone Beds from the Upper Cretaceous Two Medicine Formation of Montana: Taphonomic and Biologic Implications," *Canadian Journal of Earth Sciences*, vol. 30, 1993, pp. 997–1006.

10. James O. Farlow and Michael K. Brett-Surman, eds., *The Complete Dinosaur* (Bloomington, Ind.: Indiana University Press, 1997), pp. 499–501; Weishampel, Dodson, and Osmólska, p. 43.

11. Edwin H. Colbert, R. B. Cowles, and C. M. Bogert, "Temperature Tolerances in the American Alligator and their Bearing on the Habits, Evolution, and Extinction of the Dinosaurs," *American Museum of Natural History Bulletin 86*, 1946, pp. 327–374.

12. Currie and Padian, p. 664.

13. John H. Ostrom, "The Evidence for Endothermy in Dinosaurs," *A Cold Look at the Warm-Blooded Dinosaurs* (Washington, D.C.: American Association for the Advancement of Science, *Selected Symposium no. 28*, 1980), pp. 15–54.

14. R. McNeill Alexander, *Dynamics of Dinosaurs & Other Extinct Giants* (New York: Columbia University Press, 1989), p. 43.

15. Ibid., pp. 40–41.

16. Paul, pp. 141–147; Robert T. Bakker, *The Dinosaur Heresies* (New York: William Morrow and Company, 1986), p. 218.

17. Author interview with John H. Ostrom, 1989.

18. James O. Farlow, Matt B. Smith, and John M. Robinson, "Body Mass, Bone 'Strength Indicator,' and Cursorial Potential of *Tyrannosaurus rex*," *Journal of Vertebrate Paleontology*, vol. 15, 1995, pp. 713–725.

19. Kenneth Carpenter and Philip J. Currie, eds., *Dinosaur Systematics* (Cambridge, England: Cambridge University Press, 1990), pp. 88, 102–104.

20. Carpenter and Currie, p. 141.

Chapter 6. Eggs and Babies

1. Kenneth Carpenter, Karl F. Hirsch, and John R. Horner, eds., *Dinosaur Eggs and Babies* (Cambridge, England: Cambridge University Press, 1994), pp. 15–30.

2. Dong Zhi-Ming and Philip J. Currie, "On the Discovery of an Oviraptorid Skeleton on a Nest of Eggs at Bayan Mandahu, Inner Mongolia, People's Republic of China," *Canadian Journal of Earth Science*, vol. 33., 1996, pp. 631–636.

3. Carpenter, Hirsch, and Horner, p. 1.

4. Kenneth Carpenter and Thom Holmes (ed.) "A Dinosaur Embryo from the Land of Dragons," *Dino Times*, October 1996, p. 1.

5. Carpenter, Hirsch, and Horner, p. 37.

6. Gregory S. Paul, *Predatory Dinosaurs of the World* (New York: Simon and Schuster, 1988), p. 42.

7. Mark A. Norell, J. M. Clark, Luis M. Chiappe, and D. Dashzeveg, "A Nesting Dinosaur," *Nature*, vol. 378, 1995, pp. 774–776.

Chapter 7. Feeding Habits and Adaptations

1. John R. Horner and Don Lessem, *The Complete T. rex* (New York: Simon & Schuster, 1993), p. 206.

2. Philip J. Currie and Kevin Padian, eds., *The Encyclopedia of Dinosaurs* (San Diego, Calif.: Academic Press, 1997), p. 736.

3. Gregory M. Erickson, Samuel D. van Kirk, Jinntung Su, Marc E. Levenston, William E. Caler, and Dennis R. Carter, "Bite-Force Estimation For *Tyrannosaurus Rex* From Tooth-Marked Bones," *Nature*, vol. 382, 1996, pp. 706-708.

4. Author interview with Philip J. Currie, April 1999.

5. Thomas R. Holtz, Jr., "Predation in T. rex and Other Theropods," The Dinosaur Mailing List, n.d., dinosaur@usc.edu (November 29, 1994).

6. David M. Unwin, A. Perle, and C. Trueman, "*Protoceratops* and *Velociraptor* Preserved in Association: Evidence for Predatory Behavior in Dromaeosaurid Dinosaurs," *The Journal of Vertebrate Paleontology*, vol. 15, supplement to no. 3, 1995, pp. 57A–58A.

7. Gregory S. Paul, *Predatory Dinosaurs of the World* (New York: Simon and Schuster, 1988), p. 38.

8. Ibid.

9. Edwin H. Colbert, *The Little Dinosaurs of Ghost Ranch* (New York: Columbia University Press, 1995), p. 109.

10. Report of a Philip J. Currie lecture in Seattle Wash., The Dinosaur Mailing List, n.d., dinosaur@usc.edu (May 24, 1999).

11. Thom Holmes, participant in the Argentinean-Canadian Dinosaur Project in 1999. The bones were excavated in 1997 through 1999 and are being studied by Philip J. Currie of the Royal Tyrrell Museum of Palaeontology in Drumheller, Alberta, Canada, and Rodolfo A. Coria of the Carmen Funes Municipal Museum in Plaza Huincul, Neuquén, Argentina.

12. Author interview with Michael Balsai, University of Pennsylvania, October 11, 1999.

13. Horner and Lessem, pp. 213–214.

14. Karen Chin, Timothy T. Tokaryk, Gregory M. Erickson, and Lewis C. Calk, "A King-Sized Theropod Coprolite," *Nature*, vol. 393, 1998, pp. 680–682.

15. Gregory M. Erickson, "Breathing Life Into *Tyrannosaurus rex*," *Scientific American*, September 1999, p. 47.

16. Karen Chin, "Exceptional Soft-Tissue Preservation in a Theropod Coprolite from the Upper Cretaceous Dinosaur Park Formation of Alberta," *Journal of Vertebrate Paleontology, Abstracts of Papers*, vol. 19, supplement to no. 3, September 14, 1999, pp. 37A–38A.

17. Tim Gardom with Angela Milner, *The Book of Dinosaurs* (Rocklin, Calif.: Prima Publishing, 1993), p. 113.

18. Alan J. Charig and Angela Milner, "*Baryonyx*, a Remarkable New Theropod Dinosaur," *Nature*, vol. 324, 1986, pp. 359–361.

19. David J. Varricchio, "Gut Contents for a Cretaceous Tyrannosaur: Implications for Theropod Dinosaur Digestive Tracts," *Journal of Vertebrate Paleontology, Abstracts of Papers*, vol. 19, supplement to no. 3, September 14, 1999, p. 82A.

20. Edwin H. Colbert, *Dinosaurs, Their Discovery and Their World* (New York: E. P. Dutton, 1961), p. 65.

Chapter 8. Extinction of the Dinosaurs

1. Philip J. Currie and Kevin Padian, eds., *The Encyclopedia of Dinosaurs* (San Diego, Calif.: Academic Press, 1997), p. 221.

2. David M. Raup, *Extinction: Bad Genes or Bad Luck* (New York: W. W. Norton, 1991), p. 71.

Chapter 9. Major Theropod Discoveries

1. William B. Gallagher, *When Dinosaurs Roamed New Jersey* (New Brunswick, N.J.: Rutgers University Press, 1997), p. 38.

2. Thomas H. Huxley, "On the Animals Which are Most Nearly Intermediate Between Birds and Reptiles," *Geology Magazine*, vol. 5, 1868, pp. 357–365.

3. Joseph Wallace, *The American Museum of Natural History's Book of Dinosaurs and Other Ancient Creatures* (New York: Simon & Schuster, 1994), p. 111; Helen J. McGinnis, *Carnegie's Dinosaurs* (Pittsburgh, Penn.: The Carnegie Institute, 1982), p. 103.

4. Personal communication with Phil Currie.

5. Mark A. Norell et al., "A Theropod Dinosaur Embryo and the Affinities of the Flaming Cliffs Dinosaur Eggs," *Science*, vol. 266, pp. 779–782.

6. David M. Unwin, A. Perle, and C. Trueman, "*Protoceratops* and *Velociraptor* Preserved in Association: Evidence for Predatory Behavior in Dromaeosaurid Dinosaurs," *The Journal of Vertebrate Paleontology*, vol. 15, supplement to no. 3, 1995, pp. 57A–58A.

7. Xi-Jin Zhao and Philip J. Currie, "A Large Crested Theropod from the Jurassic of Xinjiang, People's Republic of China," *Canadian Journal of Earth Sciences*, vol. 30, October–November 1993, pp. 2027–2036.

8. Mark A. Norell, J. M. Clark, Luis M. Chiappe, and D. Dashzeveg, "A Nesting Dinosaur," *Nature*, vol. 378, 1995, pp. 774–776.

9. Kenneth Carpenter and Thom Holmes (ed.) "A Dinosaur Embryo from the Land of Dragons," *Dino Times*, October 1996, p. 1.

10. Chen Pei-Ji, Dong Zhi-Ming, and Zhen Shuo-Nan, "An Exceptionally Well-Preserved Theropod Dinosaur from the Yixian Formation of China," *Nature*, vol. 391, 1998, pp. 147–152.

11. Ji Qiang, Philip J. Currie, Mark A. Norell, and Ji Shu-An, "Two Feathered Dinosaurs from Northeastern China," *Nature*, vol. 393, 1998, pp. 753–761.

GLOSSARY

archosaur—The group of reptiles that included dinosaurs, pterosaurs (extinct flying reptiles), and crocodiles.

bilateral symmetry—A feature of vertebrate body design in which one side of the body is a mirror image of the other.

bipedal—Walking on two legs.

braincase—The internal portion of the skull that encloses and protects the brain.

carnivore—A meat-eating creature.

cast—To make an exact replica of the original using a mold.

caudal—Pertaining to the tail.

cervical—Pertaining to the neck.

chordate—An animal with a backbone, including one with the precursor of the backbone called the notochord.

classification—A traditional system of classifying organisms based on their similarities in form. The hierarchy of this classification method is kingdom, phylum, class, order, family, genus, species.

coprolite—Fossilized animal dung.

Cretaceous Period—The third and final major time division of the Mesozoic Era (144 to 65 million years ago). The end of the age of dinosaurs.

denticle—Small tooth or toothlike process on a large structure.

dorsal—Pertaining to the back.

evolution—The pattern of change through time of living organisms.

extinction—The irreversible elimination of an entire species of plant or animal.

hadrosaur—A plant-eating dinosaur with a long flat snout and often a crested skull.

herbivore—A plant-eating creature.

Jurassic Period—The second of the three major time divisions of the Mesozoic Era (208 to 144 million years ago).

manus—The hand or forefoot.

Mesozoic Era—The age of reptiles spanning from 245 to 65 million years ago. Dinosaurs lived during the era from about 225 to 65 million years ago.

mosasaur—An aquatic fish-eating or shellfish-eating reptile with a deep, flat-sided tail. It was related to lizards, not dinosaurs.

nares—The openings of the nose.

olfactory—Pertaining to the sense of smell.

optic—Pertaining to vision.

orbit—The eye socket.

Ornithischia—One of two orders of dinosaurs grouped by hip structure. Ornithischians had a hip with a backward-pointing pubis bone.

ornithopods—A group of two-footed plant-eating dinosaurs.

paleontologist—A scientist who studies life-forms of the geologic past, especially through the analysis of plant and animal fossils.

pelvis—The hipbones.

pes—The hind foot.

plesiosaur—A marine reptile of the Mesozoic Era that had a squat body, paddles as limbs, and either a long neck and small head or a short neck and large head.

predator—A creature that kills other creatures for food.

pterosaur—A flying reptile that lived during the Mesozoic Era.

pubis—One of the three hip bones.

quadrupedal—Walking on four legs.

raptor—Popular nickname for any member of the group of dromaeosaur theropods. Raptors are noted for the large retractable killing claw on the second toe of each foot.

Saurischia—One of two orders of dinosaurs grouped by hip structure. Saurischians had a hip with a forward-pointing pubis bone.

sauropod—Large, plant-eating dinosaurs with long necks and long tails.

talons—Claws that could be used to catch or tear open prey.

thecodont—One of the groups of reptiles that lived during the Triassic Period.

theropods—A group of saurischian dinosaurs that ate meat and walked on two legs.

Triassic Period—The first of the three major time divisions of the Mesozoic Era (245 to 208 million years ago).

vertebra—A bone of the neck, spine, or tail.

vertebrate—Any animal that has a backbone (spine).

FURTHER READING

Even though there have been hundreds of books about dinosaurs published, reputable dinosaur books are hard to find. Listed here are some of the authors' favorites. They range from the examination of individual kinds of dinosaurs to several encyclopedic volumes covering a wide range of dinosaur-related topics. A number of history books are included in the list as well to help those who are interested in the lives and times of paleontologists.

Bakker, Robert T. *The Dinosaur Heresies*. New York: William Morrow and Company, 1986.
This highly entertaining and colorful account of the days and lives of dinosaurs is rich with both scientific fact and speculation. Bakker provides his own marvelous and lively illustrations.

Colbert, Edwin H. *The Great Dinosaur Hunters and Their Discoveries*. New York: Dover Publications, 1968/1984.
A classic book about the history of dinosaur discovery from the early nineteenth century to the Arctic explorations of the 1960s.

———. *The Little Dinosaurs of Ghost Ranch*. New York: Columbia University Press, 1995.
The engrossing story of Colbert's involvement in excavating a fossil-rich site of Coelophysis specimens in New Mexico during the late 1940s. Hundreds of specimens from this location make this theropod one of the best known from the standpoint of fossil evidence.

Dixon, Dougal, Barry Cox, R. J. G. Savage, and Brian Gardiner. *The Macmillan Illustrated Encyclopedia of Dinosaurs and Other Prehistoric Animals.* New York: Macmillan, 1988.
A comprehensive overview of dinosaurs and other fossil vertebrates with easy-reference time lines throughout.

Farlow, James O., and Michael K. Brett-Surman (eds.). *The Complete Dinosaur.* Bloomington, Ind.: Indiana University Press, 1997.
A comprehensive encyclopedia arranged by topics such as "The Discovery of Dinosaurs," "The Study of Dinosaurs," and "Biology of the Dinosaurs." Contributions are by leading experts in the field.

Farlow, James O., and Ralph E. Molnar. *The Great Hunters: Meat-Eating Dinosaurs and Their World.* New York: Franklin Watts, 1995.
A book for younger readers detailing the lifestyle of meat-eating dinosaurs.

Felber, Eric P., Philip J. Currie, and Jan Sovak. *A Moment in Time with Albertosaurus.* Calgary, Alberta, Canada: Troodon Productions, 1998.
A book for younger readers depicting the lifestyle of Albertosaurus, a relative of Tyrannosaurus.

Gallagher, William B. *When Dinosaurs Roamed New Jersey.* New Brunswick, N. J.: Rutgers University Press, 1997.
Prior to the widespread discovery of dinosaurs in the North American West, New Jersey was the mecca of dinosaur science on this continent. Paleontologist Gallagher is still searching for dinosaurs in New Jersey and provides a lively and accessible account of dinosaurs and other important fossils found in the Garden State.

Holmes, Thom. *Fossil Feud: The Rivalry of the First American Dinosaur Hunters*. Parsippany, N. J.: Julian Messner, 1998.
The true story of two rival nineteenth-century American dinosaur scientists, Edward Drinker Cope of Philadelphia and Othniel Charles Marsh of New Haven. Their bitter rivalry to find the most dinosaurs ignited dinosaur science in the latter half of the 1800s.

Horner, John R., and Don Lessem. *The Complete T. Rex*. New York: Simon and Schuster, 1993.
Written with celebrated dinosaur scientist John "Jack" Horner, this book takes an up-close-and-personal look at the most famous dinosaur of all time, Tyrannosaurus rex, *from the discovery of its bones to conjecture about its lifestyle.*

Norell, Mark A., Eugene S. Gaffney, and Lowell Dingus. *Discovering Dinosaurs*. New York: Alfred A. Knopf, 1995.
Excellent question-and-answer book from the American Museum of Natural History, home of the world's largest collection of dinosaur fossils.

Norman, David. *The Illustrated Encyclopedia of Dinosaurs*. London: Salamander Books, 1985.
Richly illustrated and comprehensive encyclopedia for all ages.

Paul, Gregory S. *Predatory Dinosaurs of the World*. New York: Simon and Schuster, 1988.
A comprehensive account of all the theropod dinosaurs.

Russell, Dale A. *The Dinosaurs of North America: An Odyssey in Time*. Minocqua, Wisc.: NorthWord Press, 1989.
An elegant examination of dinosaurs and the world in which they lived, richly illustrated with contemporary photographs of dinosaur fossil sites. It is one of the best books available that describes the environment of the dinosaurs.

Spalding, David A. *Dinosaur Hunters.* Rocklin, Calif.: Prima Publishing, 1993.

The history of dinosaur science as seen through the work of its most famous contributors. This book is a good complement to Colbert's Great Dinosaur Hunters and Their Discoveries *and covers many developments since Colbert's history in 1968.*

Sternberg, Charles H. *Life of a Fossil Hunter.* New York: Dover, 1990.

A reprint of the original 1909 memoir by one of paleontology's most famous fossil collectors. Sternberg worked for both Cope and Marsh during his long and illustrious career.

Weishampel, David B., and Luther Young. *Dinosaurs of the East Coast.* Baltimore, Md.: Johns Hopkins University Press, 1996.

The history of dinosaur discovery in the eastern half of North America is explored through this fascinating book combining science, history, and the results of new research into North America's dinosaur heritage.

INTERNET ADDRESSES

American Museum of Natural History. *Fossil Halls.* n.d. <http://www.amnh.org/exhibitions/Fossil_Halls/index.html>.

Denver Museum of Nature and Science. Use Search area to locate various Dinosaur projects. <http://www.dmns.org/>.

Discovery Communications, Inc. *Valley of the T. rex.* © 2000. <http://dsc.discovery.com/convergence/trex/trex.html>.

Jacobson, Russ. *Dino Russ's Lair: Dinosaur and Vertebrate Paleontology Information.* July 25, 2000. <http://www.isgs.uiuc.edu/dinos/dinos_home.html).

National Geographic Society. *Dinosaur Eggs.* © 1996. <http://www.nationalgeographic.com/dinoeggs/>.

The Natural History Museum, London. *Dinosaur Data Files.* © 1994–2000. <http://www.nhm.ac.uk/education/online/dinosaur_data_files.html>.

Scotese, Christopher R. *Paleomap Project.* August 8, 2000. <http://www.scotese.com>.

Summer, Edward. *The Dinosaur Interplanetary Gazette.* April 22, 2000. <http://www.dinosaur.org/frontpage.html>.

University of Bristol. *Dinobase.* n.d. <http://palaeo.gly.bris.ac.uk/dinobase/dinopage.html> (August 25, 2000).

University of California, Berkeley, Museum of Paleontology. *The Dinosauria: Truth Is Stranger than Fiction.* © 1994–2000. <http://www.ucmp.berkeley.edu/diapsids/dinosaur.html> (August 25, 2000).

INDEX